S0-ANN-055

OIL, ECONOMIC DEVELOPMENT AND DIVERSIFICATION IN BRUNEI DARUSSALAM

STUDIES IN THE ECONOMIES OF EAST AND SOUTH-EAST ASIA

General Editors: Peter Nolan, Lecturer in the Faculty of Economics and Politics, University of Cambridge, and Fellow and Director of Studies in Economics, Jesus College, Cambridge, England; and Malcolm Falkus, Professor of Economic History, University of New England, Armidale, New South Wales, Australia

In the last decades of the twentieth century the small and medium-sized nations of East and South-East Asia have begun a process of potentially enormous political and economic transformation. Explosive growth has occurred already in many parts of the region, and the more slowly-growing countries are attempting to emulate this vanguard group. The impact of the region upon the world economy has increased rapidly and is likely to continue to do so in the future.

In order to understand better economic developments within this vast and diverse region, this series aims to publish books on both contemporary and historical issues. It includes works both by Western scholars and by economists from countries within the region.

Oil, Economic Development and Diversification in Brunei Darussalam

Mark Cleary
Senior Lecturer in Geographical Sciences
University of Plymouth

and

Shuang Yann Wong
Lecturer in Geography
Nanyang Technological University
Singapore

St. Martin's Press

© Mark Cleary and Shuang Yann Wong 1994

All rights reserved. No reproduction, copy or transmission of
this publication may be made without written permission.

No paragraph of this publication may be reproduced, copied or
transmitted save with written permission or in accordance with
the provisions of the Copyright, Designs and Patents Act 1988,
or under the terms of any licence permitting limited copying
issued by the Copyright Licensing Agency, 90 Tottenham Court
Road, London W1P 9HE.

Any person who does any unauthorised act in relation to this
publication may be liable to criminal prosecution and civil
claims for damages.

First published in Great Britain 1994 by
THE MACMILLAN PRESS LTD
Houndmills, Basingstoke, Hampshire RG21 2XS
and London
Companies and representatives
throughout the world

A catalogue record for this book is available
from the British Library.

ISBN 0–333–59554–8

Printed in Great Britain by
Ipswich Book Co Ltd
Ipswich, Suffolk

First published in the United States of America 1994 by
Scholarly and Reference Division,
ST. MARTIN'S PRESS, INC.,
175 Fifth Avenue,
New York, N.Y. 10010

ISBN 0–312–12113–X

Library of Congress Cataloging-in-Publication Data
Cleary, Mark, 1954–
Oil, economic development, and diversification in Brunei
Darussalam / Mark Cleary and Shuang Yann Wong.
p.   cm. — (Studies in the economies of East and South-East
Asia)
Includes bibliographical references and index.
ISBN 0–312–12113–X
1. Brunei—Economic conditions.   2. Petroleum industry and trade–
–Brunei. 3. Gas industry—Brunei. 4. Diversification in industry–
–Brunei.   I. Wong, Shuang Yann.   II. Title.   III. Series.
HC445.85.C58   1994
338.95955—dc20   93–44270
                                                        CIP

Contents

List of Figures

List of Tables

Acknowledgements

A number of individuals and institutions have helped in the preparation of this book. The authors would particularly like to thank several government departments in Brunei Darussalam for providing data, information and advice. Particular thanks also are due to Dick Bedford, Simon Francis, Geoffrey Gunn and Kam Tin Seong for their help and support. Thanks are also due to the University of Waikato, New Zealand, for financial help towards the completion of the research for this book.

MARK CLEARY
SHUANG YANN WONG

Note

The shorter name, Brunei, rather than Negara Brunei Darussalam, has been used throughout this book solely in the interests of brevity. Unless otherwise noted in the text, currency figures are in Brunei dollars.

1 Introduction

This book is about the nature of economic growth and development in one of the smallest — and richest — states in the world, Negara Brunei Darussalam (henceforth Brunei). A micro-state, physically divided into two separate territories, the development and character of its economy and society has been intimately bound up with the growth of the hydro-carbon industry in the state, with one company, Royal Dutch–Shell, dominating the production and marketing of the state's oil and gas prod-ucts. If, as Sampson (1988, 11) has suggested, the role of the oil com-pany is 'in political and human terms, one of the oddest stories in contemporary history', this is certainly the case for Brunei and its oil industry. But, rather than seeking to provide a company history of Royal Dutch–Shell in Brunei, the focus of the book is somewhat wider. In seeking to examine the linkages between oil, economic development and diversification, it aims both to provide an informed account of the ways in which government has sought to manage oil revenues and develop the Brunei economy, and to raise some more general issues regarding the relationships between resource development and eco-nomic growth.

For academics and visitors alike, Brunei remains a country of some-times bewildering paradoxes. From the high technology, multinational installations of the oil industry along the coast, a short drive reveals a landscape of shifting cultivation, longhouse communities and, further inland, virgin tropical rainforest. Similarly, the bustle and traffic jams of the capital, Bandar Seri Begawan, frames a large, vibrant water village, Kampong Ayer, in which a sense of traditional Malay life remains amongst the paraphenalia of consumer durables. Alongside the banking, commercial and retailing developments of the last decade, the gold-topped dome and minaret of the Sultan Omar Ali Saiffudin Mosque serves to reiterate the central importance of Islam in the political and social life of the country.

A wish to explore at least some of these paradoxes underlies this book. Any examination of the nature and evolution of Brunei's economy and society needs, it is argued, to be rooted in a consideration of a number of broader issues such as development sustainability, resource conservation, employment creation, the provision of social welfare

1

benefits and political stability. In addition, the specific organisation and foci of national development plans themselves are also significant issues.

It should be noted at the outset that the researcher is inevitably constrained by the availability and nature of source material on Brunei. Government publications, the local and regional press, interviews and secondary sources have been used in this book. The use of published and government material is problematic in a number of senses. First, it is rarely as comprehensive as one would wish. Information on the detailed financial circumstances of the state, on national accounts, input-output data, or on trading data is not always available. This is especially so in relation to questions concerning investment policies and returns. Secondly, it can be difficult to obtain up-to-date information; long time-lags exist between the collation and publication of material. Thirdly, the national press and television media are subject to varying degrees of government control. The *Borneo Bulletin*, an important source of information and opinion, is owned by QAF Holdings, in which the royal family has significant equity. The weekly *Pelita Brunei* and the *Brunei Darussalam Newsletter* are the two official outlets for the dissemination of government policies and programmes to the public. None of these can truly be regarded as publications reflecting the full range of public opinion in the state. It is thus appropriate at this juncture to emphasise that caution is needed in examining both the statistical and policy-oriented sources that have informed this book. Where real difficulties exist in interpretation and evaluation these are noted in the text.

1.1   OBJECTIVES

A first objective is to examine the development of the oil industry in Brunei and to focus on the linkages between that industry and the development of Brunei's economy and society. Chapter 2 provides an account of the historical evolution of Brunei from a position as one of the more powerful Islamic city-states in the region in the 16th century, to its establishment as a British Residency in 1906 after a long period of territorial and political decline in the 19th century. The chapter outlines the political, social and economic context out of which the oil industry emerged. Commercial quantities of oil were discovered at Seria in 1929. By the late 1930s, oil provided over 80 per cent of all exports by value;

in 1991 the equivalent figure was well over 90 per cent. As Chapter 3 emphasises, the evolution of the oil industry — its technical capacity, output, institutional organisation and socio-economic linkages — has shaped the economy of the state and largely determined the nature of its development problems.

Secondly, the book will explore the impact that burgeoining oil revenues have had on a range of development strategies. As Neary and van Wijnebergen (1986) have argued, massive revenue influxes following commodity booms can have damaging effects on long-term development programmes. The development of so-called 'Dutch disease' effects, a bloated public sector, and the rise of non-productive social expenditure can all have serious implications for development planners. Brunei's development strategies, especially in the post-1974 period, can profitably be examined with reference to these broader perspectives. Chapter 4 examines some of these questions and suggests that the experience of Brunei may be of some relevance to other small, resource-rich countries which experience commodity booms. One of the central strategies of such countries — the diversification of the economic base — is the subject of Chapter 5. Efforts to create a more diverse agricultural base, the need to reduce dependence on the public sector for employment, and the potential for developing a form of import-substitution-industrialisation are examined here.

A third objective of the book is to provide an up to date account of the economic development of Brunei, together with an outline of its role in the Southeast Asian region. Brunei is a tiny country but is not without political or economic significance. It has played a full role in the Association of Southeast Asian Nations since becoming a member in 1984. Whilst it is a very small player on the world hydrocarbon market, its revenues provide it with some leverage on international investment markets. The social, cultural and political conditions in Brunei are also, it is argued, of some interest. As with a number of other Islamic nations, tensions between moderate and fundamentalist movements, coupled with pressures for increased materialism, create potential instabilities. In this respect the desire to use oil and gas revenues to secure a stable society and economy means that development strategies cannot be divorced from wider considerations of the political economy of the state. Such linkages, coupled with the beginnings of an attempt to shape avowedly Islamic development models, are examined in Chapter 4 and Chapter 6.

1.2   THE STUDY OF OIL AND DEVELOPMENT

Studies of the oil industry and of its impact on a range of economic and social development issues have been both numerous and diverse. The story of the creation, expansion and consolidation of the major oil companies in the world makes for exciting history: the work of Sampson (1988), for example, focuses on what he calls the 'Seven Sisters' that dominate the oil business worldwide, whilst Yergin's 'The Prize' (1991) graphically charts the rise of the oil industry, its influence on western capitalism and business methods, and the emergence of what he calls 'hydrocarbon man'. Company histories provide an important primary source for such studies. The classic studies of, for example, Royal Dutch (Gerretson, 1958), or British Petroleum (Longhurst, 1959; Corley, 1985) typify such works; for Brunei, Harper's (1975) monograph provides the only reasonably detailed account of the first forty years or so of oil exploration in the state.

The strategic and technical aspects of the oil industry constitutes a second thread of writing on the subject. This ranges over a wide area. Studies such as those of the Energy Information Administration, the Commodity Reports of official bodies such as the World Bank and United Nations and reports by commercial agencies such as the Economist Intelligence Unit provide background information on resources, reserves and the technical capacity of different fields as well as a bank of oil price data. In addition, volumes such as those of Jones (1988) or Sinclair (1984) provide insights into the economics of oil production, processing and marketing.

Regional studies have also been carried out to provide specific information on the distribution and production trends of oil and gas resources and reserves. Thus Shankar Sharma (1991) has considered resource trends for the Asia-Pacific region whilst a number of national studies have examined resources, mining and company structures in, for example, Burma (Corley, 1985), Indonesia (Anderson, 1972; Ooi, 1982), Malaysia (Rozali, 1987) and Singapore (Shankar Sharma, 1989).

The political economy of oil and gas has also elicited a considerable literature, admittedly, heavily biased towards the Middle East. General works such as Banks (1987) provide valuable background material to more specific works. Thus Cook (1970) gives a useful account of both the economic history of the Middle East and, more particularly, case studies on the transition of oil producing countries into rentier states.

Peterson's (1983) work examined the nature of interdependence between oil producers in the Middle East and the major, western, consumers. Giacomo (1984) further identified the important geopolitical role of the Middle East in particular, and oil-producing countries generally. The role of oil in both domestic and international political economies has been examined by Ali (1987) and Liesl (1990).

Odell's classic, *Oil and World Power* (1979), brought into sharp focus the strategic implications of oil. Two dimensions have been especially important. The extent to which geopolitical strategy has had to change to take account of the shifting power of OPEC countries in periods of oil shortage provides one area of work. As Venn (1986) has suggested, for both the historical and contemporary period, a veritable 'oil diplomacy' has emerged within the major political powers in the world. A second area concerns the extent to which disputes over both onshore and offshore boundaries, usually focused on potential hydrocarbon reserves, have the power to cause territorial conflicts. Within Southeast Asia, the work of Siddayao (1980a; 1980b) and Valencia (1985) has highlighted potential flare-up zones in the region. The dispute over the ownership of the Spratly Islands provides a contemporary example of such difficulties.

It is in the third area of writing about the oil industry — the links between oil and development — that this book may be most conveniently placed Much of that work relates most closely to studies of the impact of oil price rises on economic development strategy, and, in geographical terms, has focused largely on the Middle East. The work of Gelb and Associates (1988) and Neary and Van Wijnbergen (1988) in particular has provided a valuable theoretical and empirical context for assessing the impact of revenue boosts in the economies of small, undiversified states such as Brunei. Regional studies such as those of Crystal (1990), Looney (1991) and Stevens (1982) from the Middle East, have also sought to examine the effects of oil price booms on development strategy. Linked to this work is the attempt made in this book to document some of the fiscal and macro-economic effects of the post-1974 oil price changes within Brunei.

Conceptually akin to the above works have been a number of regional studies which have sought to place developments in oil (production, upstream and downstream processing, conservation, pricing) within overall development strategies. In this context, work done on Middle Eastern economies has been especially useful. The question of sustainability and diversification is central to El Azhary's (1984) account of development in the Gulf whilst for Abdul Rahman Osama (1987, 54) 'huge wealth and small population are the very factors which obstruct development' in the Middle East. Such a paradox applies *a fortiori* to the case of Brunei. Some work has been done on examining such issues in Southeast Asia. In an important volume dealing with the petroleum industry in Indonesia, Arief (1982) sought to develop a quantitative model of the macro-economic impact of oil revenues. Data for Brunei has proved inadequate for developing such a model. In addition, Sorab Sadri (1991) has provided a valuable perspective on the impacts of oil in some of the regional economies (Malaysia, Indonesia).

There has been very little work on Brunei on such issues. Sritua Arief (1986) provided a useful outline of economic development and planning whilst more recently, in Sadri's (1991) edited volume, Hon Kong Tse and Fernandes examined some aspects of the oil-development linkages. In addition, Hamzah (1980; 1992) has sought to examine the oil economy of the state and his later volume in particular, provides invaluable references to some of the more technical aspects of royalties and petroleum pricing in the state.

1.3　BRUNEI: AN OUTLINE OF THE COUNTRY

The state of Brunei Darussalam is located on the north-west coast of Borneo between latitudes 4 and 5.30 north of the Equator. It has a total area of some 5,765 sq.km. The state is non-contiguous and is divided into four districts: Temburong, which is largely tropical forest, Brunei-Muara, where the majority of the population is located, Tutong, a chiefly rural district, and Belait, where the major onshore oil installations are located. The capital of the state, Bandar Seri Begawan, and the oil towns of Seria and Kuala Belait are the main urban centres; Tutong and Bangar are the other district centres. The capital has experienced marked physical and demographic expansion in recent years. The growth of public sector employment, the expansion of public housing, retailing malls and sporting and cultural facilities has greatly increased the urban area. Close to 100,000 people now live in the urban region which extends almost as far as Muara. The Temburong District is divided from the rest of the state by the Limbang district of Sarawak, part of the Malaysian Federation (Figure 1.1).

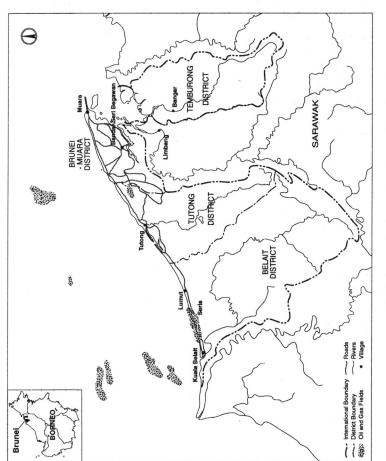

Figure 1.1   Brunei: towns and major administrative districts (scale: 1cm = 15km)

Much of the state is low-lying alluvial land with often-extensive areas of mangrove fringing the coastal belt. Inland, the Tutong, Teraja and Temburong Highlands form a largely inaccessible border area with Sarawak. The state has an equatorial climate with daily temperatures between about 24 C and 32 C. Most rainfall occurs between September and January and relative humidity rarely falls below about 80 per cent. Much of Brunei is covered by largely untouched tropical rainforest formations. Oil revenues have meant that, unlike neighbouring Sarawak and Sabah, there has been relatively little logging. The Temburong District, in particular, has large areas of forest, rich in flora and fauna, which has provided an important locale for a range of international rainforest research in recent years, coordinated by Universiti Brunei Darussalam and the Royal Geographical Society in London. The coastal belt also has extensive areas of land formerly under shifting cultivation known as *belukar* (Franz, 1980). Areas of this vegetation, together with extensive strands of abandoned rubber trees, a reflection of the decline of agriculture in the state, typify the lowland landscape of the state.

Geologically, the state is highly complex with rapid lateral and vertical changes in rock type. Of particular importance are depositional deposits laid down since the Miocene. A series of basins contain the major oil, gas and coal-bearing sediments that constitute the wealth of the country (Quazi Abdul Halim, 1992). Alongside the extensive hydrocarbon deposits a range of other resources are available. Extensive gravel deposits in the Temburong have been heavily quarried as have beach and river sand deposits. The greatly increased pace of construction work in recent years has accentuated demand. There are also important silica sands in the Tutong district which could provide the basis for glass-making in the state. Coal occurs in the Belait district and around the Brunei river but has not been mined for some decades.

Brunei has a small but rapidly growing population (Table 1.1) with average annual growth rates over the last decade in excess of 3 per cent. Ethnically three major groups are distinguished in the census (Neville, 1990). Brunei Malays are the dominant group (around 70 per cent) in 1990. The other major group is the Chinese (17 per cent in 1990). The third group, indigenous peoples, include Kedayans, Muruts, Dusuns, Belaits and Ibans. The majority of the Malays are Muslims and use the Malay language. Generally about 70 per cent of the population are Muslims, 10 per cent are Christian, 12 per cent are Buddhist and the remainder, animist and others. The Ministry of Home

Table 1.1   Population and ethnic category, 1971–90

Year	Total	Malay	Chinese	Indigenous	Others
1971	136 256	65%	23%	6%	6%
1981	192 832	65%	20%	8%	7%
1990	256 500	68%	18%	5%	9%

Source: Population Census, 1971, 1981; Population Estimates, 1990.

Affairs reported that at the end of 1990, Brunei citizens comprised about 55 per cent of the total population of Brunei. Around 10 per cent were permanent residents: many in this category would be Chinese who have to undergo strict tests to gain access to citizenship. The remaining 35 per cent are classed as temporary residents. This last category includes expatriate workers who come mainly from neighbouring ASEAN countries.

Communications, particularly with the interior districts, are difficult. The major road artery follows the coast, linking Bandar Seri Begawan with Tutong, Seria and Kuala Belait. Road communications extend across the border into Sarawak and the oil and timber town of Miri. There are smaller road networks into the Tutong and Belait districts though these are generally in poor condition. A major road links the capital with Muara which has an important deep water port facility. The country has an international air terminal with Royal Brunei Airlines and a number of other international airlines linking the state with Southeast Asia, Europe and Australia. Water is an important means of communication with the Belait, Tutong, Brunei and Temburong rivers carrying a sizeable local traffic. Motorised water taxis are an important means of transport in the capital linking the water village with the offices and commercial services on *terra firma*.

2 Brunei: From Trading City to Nation State

The achievement of formal independence in 1984 marked an important stage in the long process of national and state formation of Brunei. As one of the oldest Sultanates in the region, with a claimed royal lineage going back several hundred years, the state has a rich tradition, reflected in its customs, its social structures and its government. Such historical traditions are integral to an understanding of the nature of economic, social and political conditions in contemporary Brunei.

2.1 EARLY MODERN BRUNEI

To the first European travellers in sixteenth and seventeenth-century Borneo, the kingdom of Brunei was seen as one of the oldest and most prestigious on the island. Ruled by a Sultan claiming a long and distinguished pedigree, the capital was built on stilts on the Brunei river, its economy flourishing on the trade which animated Southeast Asia. Its royal customs and social structures bore the mark of a range of different cultural influences from Hinduism to the tenets of Islam. Archaeological work has revealed a considerable heritage of finds in the Brunei region: the caves at Niah, near the Sarawak town of Miri, have provided evidence of human occupation dating back to around 38,000 BC (Harrisson, 1970; Bellwood, 1985). Excavations within Brunei itself, whilst still at an early stage, are beginning to yield useful insights into the early development of Brunei.

At the Kota Batu site near the capital, ceramic finds suggest the possibility that the port sites of north-west Borneo carried on a considerable trade with China. Analysis of toponyms used in Chinese trading accounts also point to the probable existence of a significant trading centre in the proximity of present-day Brunei (Brown, 1970:133; Wade, 1986). Prior to the arrival of European voyagers, the Brunei region was a centre for trade. It functioned as an entrepot, exchanging the jungle products of Borneo for the silks, spices and ceramics that flowed along the trade routes from India to China. With a well developed trading

11

system in which the sea-trading captains (*nakhoda*) played an important part, Brunei certainly traded with China and with many other maritime trading cities in the region such as Malacca and Majapahit. The cultural and artefactual evidence of these linkages can be seen in the varied treasures and traditions of contemporary Brunei.

By the mid-fourteenth century, Brunei may have become sufficiently powerful to have been brought under the domination of Majapahit (Ranjit Singh, 1984, 13), and, by the late fourteenth-century, Islam may have arrived in the kingdom though the evidence is uncertain (Nicholl, 1989). The arrival of Islam undoubtedly helped to stregthen the prosperity of Brunei for Arab traders found a congenial environment within which to ply their trade. Intellectually, Islam served to further consolidate the power and institutions of the monarchy. By the late-fifteenth century, under the leadership of Sultan Bolkiah, Brunei began to expand its political and economic horizons to become the major power in the region of north-west Borneo and a city-state of some influence in the region. The fall of Malacca to the Portugese in 1511, a harbinger of European intervention in the region, led a number of Muslim merchants to shift from Malacca to Brunei; the strength of Islam in the city meant that 'the substantial extension of Brunei during the sixteenth-century was associated with the *jihad* or holy war' (Tarling, 1966:44).

When Pigafetta, the chronicler of Magellan's round the world voyage, visited the city of Brunei in 1521, the city-state was perhaps approaching the zenith of its power. His descriptions of the stilt-houses, palaces, waterways and splendour of the royal court underline the rise of the Bruneian polity and the regional significance of its economic and strategic alliances (Nicholl, 1976). The power of Brunei was based squarely on trade. The city was an entrepot, exchanging the cloths, ceramics and metals of the trading ships of the South China Sea for the much-vaunted jungle products of Borneo — camphor, ivories, hornbills, precious stones — which were in demand in regional markets. As Brown (1970:77) stresses, 'no sharp geographical boundaries of Brunei can be drawn' for the kingdom exercised control over trading networks, merchants and people rather than over large areas of territory. Control of river estuaries, a powerful presence in the ports of the region and a rich exchequer able to support an army of retainers were integral to the success of the kingdom. Certainly it controlled most of the north-west coast of Borneo, entertained relations with other Sultanates and kingdoms in the region, and had an influence extending as far as the Sulu Islands and the southern Philippines.

By the early seventeenth-century the power of Brunei was beginning to wane for a variety of reasons. Competing Sultanates — Pontianak, Banjarmasin, Sambas on Borneo and, more especially, the Sulu Sultanate in the southern Philippines, were beginning to erode the economic and political influence of Brunei. That erosion, and the subsequent fall in revenues to the Brunei rulers, weakened their ability to enforce power through the recruitment of armed retainers. As a result the power of individual nobles or *pengirans* began to eclipse that of the ruler. A second reason was the increased interest of European powers in the region. The expansion of European mercantilism in Southeast Asia was aimed largely at securing a monopoly on the high-value products of the region. Disruptions in the traditional trading patterns on Borneo (patterns which were dominated by Brunei) began to erode the economic power base of the Sultanate as the region began to be incorporated into the nascent world-economy. Much of the interest of the Dutch and, later, English trading companies centred elsewhere in the region (notably Java), but trading centres or factories were established in parts of Borneo (Succanda, Sambas, Pontianak) accentuating the steady decline in the fortunes of Brunei. By the early eighteenth-century, European travellers depicted the state as a picturesque but faded kingdom, largely bereft of its former power and influence but still proud of its royal traditions, customs and protocol.

2.2 THE 'SCRAMBLE FOR BORNEO' AND THE RESIDENCY

Whilst Brunei in particular, and Borneo generally continued to be portrayed through the nineteenth-century as regions of mystique and fantasy, a *terra incognitae* of headhunters and fabled beasts (see eg. King, 1992), the mid-nineteenth century saw a more realistic, hard-headed intervention in the region. The sea-lanes of the South China Sea took on a new significance with the growth of Singapore and Hong Kong and both Dutch and British adventurers began to explore the region and seek commercial footings, especially along the coast. With the advent of steam ships, the possibility of creating coaling-stations in the area (the island of Labuan, for example, was known to have coal deposits) also led to increased European interest. This interest was to have important, almost terminal, consequences for Brunei.

The political and economic strength of Brunei was greatly diminished by the nineteenth-century. The allegiance of the powerful nobles, or *pengirans,* to the Sultanate depended on money and, as central authority declined, so the control that the Sultanate was able to exert over its nobles weakened. Its hold over, for example, the Sulu islands or parts of south-west Borneo was always tentative; by 1800 it had virtually disappeared (Warren, 1981). The images of exoticism, products of an orientalist vision, remained strong in contemporary accounts, but concealed a court in almost terminal decline. By the late nineteenth-century, as Francis (1993) has shown, travellers' accounts portrayed this court as a picturesque and faded anachronism. This decline was further accentuated by the system of landholding in the state. Three types of holding have been identified by historians — private holdings *(tulin)*, royal holdings *(kerajaan)* and those belonging to state officers *(kuripan)* (Crisswell, 1972; Ranjit Singh, 1984). *Tulin* holdings could be disposed of quite easily without any permission; the *kerajaan* and *kuripan* holdings could be disposed of with the permission of the state council. What this meant was that in practice much of the land of the state could be sold or mortaged to outsiders. At a time when both the Sultan and many of the *pengiran* were bankrupt the temptations to sell land were great.

One of the catalysts for the contraction of the political boundaries of Brunei was the arrival of a British adventurer, James Brooke, in Sarawak. The nominal overlord of Sarawak, who owed allegiance to Brunei, Pangeran Makota, was in the throes of fighting a rebellion against his rule. In exchange for helping to suppress that rebellion, and with some encouragement from Brooke and his military friends, the Raja Muda Hassim, the power behind the throne in Brunei, offered Brooke the governorship of Sarawak in September 1841 in exchange for an annual payment of Straits $2,000. Thus the rule of the so-called 'White Rajahs' was inaugurated and the expansion of Sarawak at the expense of Brunei began (Cleary and Eaton, 1992: 48–51).

The nature of landholding in the state meant that the expansionary ambitions of the Brooke's could be accomodated, at least in part, by simply offering to buy up areas which, in one form or other, were formerly part of Brunei. Coupled with a desire to suppress piracy (which, of course, dovetailed nicely with territorial ambitions) James and his nephew Charles Brooke steadily expanded the territory of Sarawak as the Sultan of Brunei was 'forced to bargain away his kingdom in concession after concession which further reduced his chances of recovery' (Tate, 1971:177). The Brookes steadily advanced from one river basin to another: the Lupar basin (1853) for a payment of Straits $1,500 p.a., the Rajang (1861) for $4,500 p.a., the Baram (1882) for $4,200 p.a. The ultimate loss was that of the Limbang. Local unrest in the Limbang, an economically important part of Brunei and the source of much of its food supply, was used by Rajah Charles Brooke as a pretext for declaring the territory part of Sarawak in 1890. Cession money offered by Brooke was refused and Brunei did not, and does not, recognise the legality of the cession (Cleary and Shaw, 1992). More importantly, the loss of the Limbang quite literally cut Brunei in two and dealt a potentially fatal blow to its political and economic survival.

These advances from the south were paralleled by the loss of territories to the north-east. The Sultan had signed a treaty with the United States in 1850 giving the country special privileges. Whilst this meant little in practice, an American Consul, Charles Lee Moses was able to secure a ten-year lease over much of north-east Borneo in 1865 in return for an annual payment of Straits $9,500. Once again, the move was facilitated by the nature of landholding in the areas of Brunei influence and by the chronic insolvency of the Sultanate (Tate, 1971). Not much was done with the lease but, after some early hesitations, the Sultan signed a new lease with an Austrian, Baron Von Overbeck, in partnership with an English businessman, Alfred Dent. Dent eventually acquired full rights to the lease in 1880 and set about establishing a mechanism for developing the territory. After some initial hesitations, the British government authorised the creation of a Chartered Company with the remit of developing what came to be called North Borneo, under the control of a Board of Directors (Black, 1983). The North Borneo Chartered Company was to govern the territory from 1881 until the establishment of the British colony of North Borneo in 1946.

Coupled with the shrinking of its territories, the economic basis of Brunei's power was being rapidly eroded. Local taxation was high and was discouraging even the production of basic foodstuffs such as rice and sago. With the decline in the authority of the Sultanate, merchants were shifting their centre of operations to the new territories of Sarawak and North Borneo. There, the possibilities of tapping into the indigenous jungle trade together with options to develop forms of plantation farming, were to provide much more attractive investment opportunities

(Cleary, 1993). With the economy in a state of collapse, trade virtually dried up. Consular reports of the period confirm this view:

> 'No foreign vessels visited Brunei during the year ... The Government of Brunei has for many years past been in a very feeble state ... trade is decidedly on the decrease' (1865)
>
> 'The principal obstacles to material progress in the country, and consequently to the development of trade, are a weak central Government, too great power in the hands of local chiefs ... and the want of capital and enterprise' (1874)
>
> 'Such trade as there was has fallen off and the steamer which called monthly from Singapore has now ceased its visits' (1900)

The attitude of both the British and Dutch governments to intervention in Borneo was equivocal. The Dutch had, by the 1850s, formally incorporated Dutch Borneo (Kalimantan) within the colonial structures established in the Dutch East Indies. But in terms of personnel and administrative structures the impress was always light: it was not until the discovery of the oil fields of East Kalimantan around the town of Balikpapan that a more coherent administration was developed (see Lindblad, 1988). Colonial rule was costly and carried political risks. The British government remained reluctant to set up formal colonies in Borneo; whilst recognising that north-west Borneo might have both strategic and economic significance, the British sought political solutions which would minimise costs to the Exchequer.

For Sarawak and North Borneo a policy of laissez-faire seemed most appropriate. Sarawak, whilst independent, was ruled by a British Raja with British administrative cadres, many of whom were former colonial administrators in India or the Malay states. Likewise the option of a Chartered Company in North Borneo gave the British government a semblance of control over affairs (the policy of the Chartered Company was, after all, subject to Parliamentary scrutiny) without the high cost of a full-blown colonial apparatus. But, as the territory of Brunei diminished, the British government was faced with a virtual race between Sarawak and North Borneo to swallow up the surviving remnants of the Sultanate. In Britain conflicts between the Foreign and Colonial Office and between pro-Brooke and pro-Company alliances led to the establishment of British Protectorates for Sarawak, North Borneo and Brunei. In September 1888 Brunei became a British Protectorate: Sultan

Hashim, suggests Tate (1971: 184), 'was content to accept the Protectorate because it was the best guarantee for the preservation of his own
dynasty and sovereignty'.

In the event the apparent territorial guarantees proved illusory; Brunei
continued to lose pieces of territory to Brooke's Sarawak and the
Chartered Company. The Padas district was lost in 1889, the Limbang in
1890 and Kinarut in 1897 and other pieces continued to disappear in
exchange for annuities and payments. A rebellion in the Belait district
in the late 1890s almost led to the loss of that area (and its rich hydrocarbon deposits !) to Sarawak (Horton, 1987). By the turn-of-the century
the country was in a parlous state: bankrupt, administratively moribund,
and threatened by the advances of Brooke and the Chartered Company.

Faced with a range of competing interests the British government
eventually decided that, rather than condoning the dismantling of
Bruneian territory and the disappearance of Brunei as a nation, it would
guarantee the borders of the state and establish a Resident in Brunei,
rather in the manner of the Residents operating in some of the Malay
states, to 'advise' the Sultan on all matters save those of religion and
customary practices. Thus, from 1906, Brunei became a Residency and
its borders and survival were guaranteed by the British. Whilst never
formally a colony, government was established under close British
scrutiny.

2.3 GOVERNMENT AND ADMINISTRATION UNDER THE RESIDENCY 1906–59

The decision to establish a Residency in Brunei did not meet with the
approval of either Brooke's Sarawak or the Chartered Company who had
hoped to be able to incorporate the remnants of Brunei in their own territories. Sultan Hashim viewed the Residency as providing some sort of
guarantee of the survival of the Kingdom. In return for 'accepting' a
Resident the Sultan and some of the leading *pengirans* were provided
with annuities and were allowed to retain control over matters relating to
religion or custom. The Resident, as a representative of the Crown,
advised the Sultan in Council on matters of finance, administration, foreign policy and defence. The British had introduced Residents to a
number of Malay states: the system, it seemed, rested on the authoritative
nature of the advice proferred: 'it does not follow, because the Resident

is only the adviser, that the ruler may reject his advice when the peace and good order of the country are at stake ... the fiction ... that the Residents are merely advisers must be kept up' (quoted in Tarling, 1993, 73). For the Sultan, the system provided a degree of security against external attacks, for Britain, it allowed Brunei to remain as a buffer between Sarawak and North Borneo at minimum cost to the Treasury.

Horton (1984; 1985) has provided the most complete and authoritative accounts of the administration of the Residency period which lasted from 1906 until the formal establishment of self-government in 1959. Two particular aspects will be highlighted here: administrative reforms and the economy. One of the most significant problems faced ¯ by the incoming administration (which was always small — the Assistant Resident together with a small staff of civil servants) was the bankruptcy of the state. McArthur's Report on Brunei in 1904 (McArthur, 1987), compiled in part to examine the options available to the British, describes the chronic insolvency of the state, the lack of any kind of administration and the poverty of its people. In particular it noted that many of the sources of state revenue (taxes, monopolies on imports and exports, duties) had been sold or mortgaged to meet immediate cash shortages. Thus monopolies on the import of opium, gambier, tobacco and kerosene had been sold off, primarily to Chinese merchants and money-lenders. Duties on a range of other products–coconut oil, sugar, brassware — were also in private hands (Table 2.1).

With the aid of a loan from the Straits Settlement, the Resident set about purchasing back as many of these monopolies as possible in order

Table 2.1   Monopolies and tax farms mortgaged by Brunei

Import duties:	on most major items, 1901–29
Export duties:	on cutch, 1906–11
	on jungle rubber, 1903–08
Import monopolies:	opium, 1901–15
	gambier, 1902–22
	coconut oil, 1902–22
	kerosene, 1902–22
	salt, 1900–10
	tobacco, 1902–17
	sugar, 1902–17

Source: McArthur (1987).

Table 2.2   Income, expenditure and debt, 1906–40

Year	Debt /% GNP	Income($)	Expenditure($)
1906	710%	28 173	145 245
1920	208%	206 253	223 690
1930	120%	333 069	373 604
1940	0	1 556 000	1 462 000

Source: Horton (1985), 167.

to secure an adequate and reliable state revenue. The institution of a poll-tax, although not entirely successful in its implementation (the Annual Reports of the period indicate considerable opposition from indigenous Kedayans) also provided some additional revenue. As conditions in Brunei became more secure, revenues from customs duties also began to flow back into the Treasury. In 1906, state income of about Straits $28,000 contrasted with expenditure of around $145,000; by 1920 income and expenditure were almost in balance with the burden of national debt (primarily the 1906 loan) greatly reduced. It is worth noting that before commercial oil came onstream in the early 1930s, the budget was largely in balance and the national debt was steadily falling (Table 2.2).

At a time when neighbouring regions (the Malay States and Straits Settlements; North Borneo; East Kalimantan) were beginning to be drawn into a world commodity market through the production of export commodities such as oil, tobacco and rubber, such developments in Brunei were conspicuous by their absence. Wallerstein (1989) has argued that the process of incorporation, a process by which an *external* region is transformed, through commodity production, into a *peripheral* region, depended crucially on firstly, the 'freeing' of land, labour and resources and, secondly, a collaborative state apparatus facilitating investment and commodity production. From the outset, the Residency sought to attract foreign investment in order to stimulate commodity production and thereby enhance state revenues. Its achievements were mixed to say the least.

To achieve these ends, efforts were made to 'free' land, labour and resources in order to stimulate investment (Cleary, 1992b). The haphazard and chronically insecure nature of pre-Residency trade meant there was little nascent merchant capital in the country which might have acted as a catalyst for investments in the production sector.

Secondly, both land and labour conditions were encumbered by a variety of constraints. The former was bound by that complex set of *tulin* linkages which inhibited the ability of the administration to provide secure lease or freehold titles to potential investors in, say, the plantation sector (Crisswell, 1972). Unlike neighbouring regions such as North Borneo (Cleary, 1992a), no Land Code had been enacted to enable secure alienation of land to proceed. Similarly labour relations were bound up with complex, local systems of indenture. Any labour supply would have to be drawn largely from outside.

The first efforts of the administration were aimed at attracting potential investors in plantation rubber. The 1906 Annual Report noted four applications for plantation land but three were soon withdrawn. The main obstacle lay in the landholding system. In 1907 a Land Code was promulgated but was difficult to implement because of opposition from the Sultan, from holders of traditional *tulin* rights and from the Kedayan shifting cultivators in interior areas. Whilst investors were active in neighbouring regions, 'they appeared to have turned a cold shoulder upon Brunei', the Resident concluded, largely because of the land problem (Annual Report, 1909). In the end, land grants were made to five British investors in 1911, with the two largest estates located in the Temburong. By 1915 the production of plantation rubber was underway; the Temburong estates imported labour from Java and India.

Alongside efforts to develop the rubber industry, the Resident sought to improve trade and general economic conditions in other areas. The production of cutch, a dyestuff manufactured from mangrove bark, expanded through to the 1920s contributing to export revenues. The coal mines at Brooketon (near the present town of Muara), though leased by the Brooke's, were an important export on which the state levied a royalty (Horton, 1986). Coal production averaged around 20,000–30,000 tons per year but the Brooke's never made much of a profit from the enterprise which ceased production in 1924. Other economically valuable products included jelutong (a form of 'wild' rubber) and traditional jungle products such as gambier. In seeking to improve the economic position of the state, the administration also enacted legislation designed to facilitate prospecting for oil. The discovery of oil in the Miri field in neighbouring Sarawak in 1911 encouraged prospecting in the Belait district. As Chapter 3 indicates, the discovery of commercial quantities of oil in 1929 was preceded by at least twenty years of prospecting, concession-trading and false starts.

Prior to the discovery of oil, the pattern of exports was dominated by rubber, cutch and by the coal extracted from the Rajah Brooke's mines at Brooketon (Figure 2.1). Rubber production fluctuated considerably with periodic crises prompted by price collapses (in 1918 and 1929 for example) affecting production in both the estate and smallholder sector. Rubber was widely grown by smallholders alongside their crops of *padi* and vegetables. Such was the interest in planting rubber trees that regulations were enacted to ensure that grants of land made to small-holders stipulated that they planted 'more homely products' alongside the ubiqitous rubber trees (Annual Report, 1917). The quality of small-holder rubber often left much to be desired: 'the latex smallholder' noted the 1917 Report, 'coagulates his latex in a kerosene tin, rolls it in a home-made mangle, dries it in the open air, and smokes it over his kitchen fire'. It is hardly suprising that such rubber failed to command the top prices in the market!

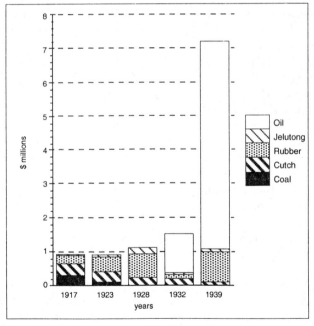

Figure 2.1   State exports by value, 1917–39

The country was a consistent rice importer, a characteristic it has retained through to the present. It would appear that well before the discovery of oil, Bruneian agriculture was languishing. The loss of the Limbang had deprived Brunei of an important rice-growing region and the country was forced to rely on imported rice. Shifting agriculture was practiced by the interior Kedayan tribes; the coastal and urban Malays preferred, as did the Chinese, to concentrate upon vegetables, fruits and, in particular, rubber. Such products had a ready market and produced better cash returns than rice.

If the first priority of government had been to establish a sound financial base, a second aim was to begin to improve the infrastructure of the state. The funds available for this were minimal. Horton (1985, 157) has noted that the administration had the princely sum of Straits $5 per person/per year in 1911 to spend on such improvements; by 1931, despite improvements in the revenue base, the figure was still less than $12. Under the circumstances not much could be done. Development had to be funded from state revenues. Much effort was devoted to public works. A programme of bridle-path construction was launched in 1919, designed to link the rubber estates in Temburong and those near the capital at Gadong and Berakas. The first car made its appearance in Brunei in 1924 and by the early 1930s a number of hard-earth roads had been created (Horton, 1988; 1990). One of the chief problems, apart from lack of money, was the absence of suitable roadstone; gravels in the Temburong river were (and remain) a good source, but the costs of extraction and transport were high.

As the oilfields around Kuala Belait developed in the early 1930s, establishing a reliable road link with the capital became a priority. As the 1933 Annual Report noted, 'with increasing traffic on the highway to the important district of Kuala Belait, a policy of metalling will have to be carried out'. Until after the Second World War, the trip had to be made largely along the beach taking due account of the tides and natural hazards of such a journey. By the late 1930s the need for better roads was clear: an annual increase of 15 per cent in motorized traffic was noted in 1936, by 1938 it was 57 per cent. The impact of the admittedly limited development programmes in the pre-war period was also felt in changes to settlement. As the oilfields expanded, a new oil-town, Seria emerged. Its regular, grid-like settlement pattern, with expatriate and local housing strictly demarcated, contrasted with indigenous towns such as Tutong. As Seria and Kuala Belait grew with the influx of Chinese oilfield workers, the old district office in the inland town of Kuala Balai, some 15 km up the Belait River, was shifted to Kuala Belait. Gradually the centre of economic gravity shifted from Brunei Town to the coastal developments at the other end of the state; a range of geographic and social changes were to accompany the rise of the oil economy.

Brunei Town itself felt the hand of change in this period. The establishment of the Residency prompted the Resident to suggest a beautification of the capital. Seeking to recreate an 'ordered', 'pleasant' and 'healthy' capital, modelled, no doubt, on the quintessential (and mythical) English country town, the administration sought to shift settlement away from the river-bound stilt houses that had long been a part of the Brunei Malay way of life, and create a settlement on *terra firma* (Cleary and Kam,1992). The 1908 report noted that 'a town site at Brunei has been laid out, two short streets made, and street lamps erected. A canal is in the course of excavation beside the main street for the use of small boats'. By 1910 a number of Chinese shopkeepers had set up in the new settlement and, over the next decade, a number of new streets were laid out. By the mid-1920s 'the appearance of the town was entirely changed and great improvements made' (Horton, 1985, 188). But the water village (Kampong Ayer) remained; by an irony of history, it survived the bombardments of 1944 relatively intact, whilst its counterpart on dry land was virtually flattened. Today's threat comes from planners rather than planes.

2.4   POST-WAR CHANGES AND THE 1959 CONSTITUTION

For most of the period 1942–1945 Brunei, along with the other Borneo states, was under the control of the Japanese. The departing British sought to disable the oilfields prior to the Japanese invasion and succeeded in at least delaying their return to production. The Japanese were able to bring oil back on stream in conditions of great difficulty; Harper (1975) suggested that some eleven and a half million barrels were mined from the adjoining Seria and Miri fields in the war years, amounting to about two years of pre-war production, a not inconsiderable achievement in the circumstances. Within two years, the installations were again largely destroyed as the Japanese withdrew and it was not until late-1945 that quantities of oil again began to flow from the field. These patterns of production are examined more fully in the next chapter.

The rapid recovery of the oilfield operations after the destruction of the Second World War meant that, as in previous years, oil revenues continued to dominate both the exports and revenues of the state. Oil production levels had outstripped their pre-war levels by 1948 and continued to rise through the 1950s peaking at about 110,000 bpd in 1957. Oil revenues (comprising mining rights and royalties together with corporation and income taxes) comprised about 75 per cent of all state revenues for most of the 1950s, falling to around 55 per cent at the end of the decade as oil production began to stagnate. It is difficult to clearly distinguish the oil and non-oil revenue contributions; revenues classified in the national accounts as pertaining to investments, for example, largely reflect the investments of oil-related surpluses in overseas portfolios. The enormous contribution of oil to national revenue remains clear. The oil price hikes of the 1970s altered only the size of these surpluses; the fundamental proportions remained constant.

In the late 1950s, when oil production from the Seria field was peaking, state surpluses were large: in 1956 around B$88 million, in 1957, B$91 million, in 1958, B$97 million. Even when allowance is made for Development Fund expenditure a considerable surplus was apparent. Brunei, then, was a rich nation with a budgetary surplus well before the events of the early-1970s in the world oil market. Alongside the oil sector, other parts of the economy were stagnant. The acreage devoted to rubber remained at around 30,000 acres for the period 1940–1960 but the quality remained poor with little replanting and increasing encroachment from urban expansion. Rubber exports produced around B$4 million in the 1950s with something of a mini-boom during the period of the Korean War. Their overall contribution to exports was, however, dwarfed by oil revenues (Table 2.3). Agricultural employment stagnated too as employment in the oil sector, construction and the public services expanded.

Table 2.3   Rubber exports, 1932–69

Years	Rubber exports ($)	—	As % of total exports
1932–9	0.697m		15.9%
1940–9	1.472m		n.a.
1950–9	3.920m		0.1%
1960–9	1.924m		0.001%

Source: Ameer Ali (1992).

The accession of Sultan Haji Omar Ali Saiffudin to the throne in June 1950 marked the start of a range of administrative, political and economic changes in Brunei (Hussainmiya, 1992). As noted above, the growth of revenues from the oilfields provided a sound financial base for a range of infrastructural and welfare services in the state. Improvements to communications, public investment in housing, the development of hospital and educational services, the expansion of scholarships for study overseas (especially in Britain), the initiation of social services (old age pensions, for example) were all hallmarks of the 1950s and 1960s. The first National Development Plans dated from this period, as the following chapter makes clear. In many ways, the accession saw the beginnings of a move towards a modern, developed, independent state (Wijeweera, 1992, 184–5).

A number of important administrative reforms were begun in this period. The inception of a national development plan has already been noted with budgetary allocations for such expenditure being made from the growing current account surplus. A tier of local administration was established with the Local Councils Enactment of 1956. These urban and rural councils had a membership nominated by the Sultan in Council and were given an annual, audited budget and responsibility for a range of functions — electricity, water supply, sanitation, recreation facilities. Revenues were to be derived from rates on property and licence fees. Alongside these local developments the public services continued to expand: the 21 government departments in 1950 had increased to 31 by 1960 with an accompanying increase in personnel from 813 to 3 442 (Wijeweera, 1992, 190).

The late 1950s saw a number of important political developments in Brunei. The creation of Local Councils under the 1956 Enactment created at least the possibility of elected positions being made available and the establishment, and official registration of the Parti Rakyat Brunei (PRB) in 1956 under the leadership of Sheik Azahari was in part a response to this. The call for direct elections to the Local Councils was rejected by Sultan Omar. During 1957 and 1958 the Sultan and his advisers were engaged in a long, intricate process of negotiation over a new Constitution for the country. Hussainmiya (1992, 164–167), has argued that the Sultan sought to establish a slow and steady shift from protectorate status to self-government and, eventually, independence at a time when most colonial governments were rapidly leaving the newly emergent nations of Asia and Africa. The slow pace of change may equally be read as an essentially conservative policy designed to ensure the central and unchallenged position of the Sultan as head of government.

The new Constitution was promulgated in September 1959. It ended the 1906 Residency agreement, returning supreme authority for all internal matters to the Sultan. The post of Resident was replaced by a High Commissioner, with Britain retaining responsibility for defence, foreign affairs and internal security (Leake, 1990, 59–60). An Executive and Legislative Council were created. The Sultan presided over the former which was called at the request of the Sultan alone. The Legislative Council was to include elected members from the District Councils, a provision which was later to create difficulties for the PRB. A key feature of the new Constitution, and one which has been given added prominence in the post-independence period, was the constitutional enshrinement of the ideology of the Malay Islamic Monarchy or MIB. As Wijeweera (1992, 189) notes: 'No person other than a "Malay professing the Muslim religion and belonging to the Shafeite sect of that religion" could hold office as Menteri Besar or State Secretary. The language of administration was to be the Malay language. In addition Islam was accorded the status of state religion and the Sultan was to be the Head of the religion of the state. Finally, the supreme executive authority of the State was to be vested in the Sultan and all exercise of authority (by others) was to be in his name and on his behalf. Thus, the three pillars of the MIB concept associated with Brunei's past were put in place, as an expression of cultural nationalism.'

The National Enactment, established in 1960 laid down the criteria for citizenship in Brunei. Whilst indigenous groups were granted full citizenship rights, members of the sizeable immigrant population (primarily the Chinese) were required to fulfill strict conditions, most notably a period of residence of 20 out of the last 25 years and passing a Malay language test. These conditions meant that the Chinese, some 20 per cent of the population, were virtually restricted to securing only rights of permanent residence, not citizenship. That position remains largely unchanged today.

2.5 TOWARDS INDEPENDENCE

With the establishment of self-government in 1959, two further issues remained significant in the changed political complexion of the state:

moves towards joining the Federation of Malaysia, and the place of the PRB in the new state. The possibility of some sort of merger between the British colonies of Sarawak, North Borneo and Brunei had been anticipated by Britain. Brunei and Sarawak had been treated by the British as a single administrative unit since 1948: officers from Sarawak were seconded to service in Brunei. Whilst the arrangement had been designed primarily to cut costs, suggestions were made by the Colonial Office that such a framework might allow for a political union between the three states. The proposals met with considerable opposition from Sultan Omar Ali and, when the 1959 Constitution was promulgated, an agreement to separate the administration of Brunei and Sarawak was also signed.

In the early 1960s the British were active in seeking to redraw the political boundaries of Malaysia and Borneo. The Malaysian Prime Minister, Tunku Abdul Rahman, had proposed the idea of a Federation of Malaysia in 1961 which would include the Borneo states of Brunei, North Borneo and Sarawak within a federal system of government. The reactions were equivocal. The British, anxious to be rid of their colonial territories, were largely enthusiastic. For Brunei the idea provoked a mixed reaction. Certainly it would have placed Brunei as part of a wider, perhaps more powerful, Muslim country with whom it had some cultural and political affinities. On the other hand, sovereignty would be lost, the oil wealth of the country dissipated and there were fears that Malaysian administration might simply replace one form of neo-colonialism with another.

The potentially volatile situation was complicated by electoral issues. The 1959 Constitution had provided for elected members in the Legislative Council, elected through four district councils: Brunei, Belait, Tutong and Temburong. Azahari's PRB fought these elections on a platform of strong opposition to the establishment of a Malaysian Federation. Instead he proposed the establishment of a united North Kalimantan (Brunei, Sarawak and North Borneo) together with internal reforms. Whilst the PRB declared its loyalty to Sultan Omar Ali, the Sultan himself felt threatened by the moves. In the August 1962 District Council elections the PRB took a large number of the seats. The elections changed the political complexion of the moves towards a federation of Malaysia. The meetings of the new Legislative Council were suspended; the PRB sought to place both Britain and the Sultan under pressure to keep Brunei out of the Federation.

In early December 1962 the PRB launched an armed revolt in Brunei which was regarded by both the Sultan and the British as a direct threat to sovereignty. Invoking the Treaty of Protection, British military assistance was called in and the revolt was quickly put down. Emergency Regulations were put in place and the activities of the Legislative Council and district councils were suspended. Elections to a new Legislative Council were made in March 1965 but no clear political parties or alliances were formed. No further elections to that body have been held through to the present.

The net effect of the revolt was three-fold. It undoubtedly nipped the bud of democratic government in the country, frustrating further attempts to establish district or national forms of elected government. Secondly, it soured relations between Brunei, the Philippines and Indonesia; the latter, in particular, was regarded as openly hostile to Brunei and relations were not fully mended until almost two decades later. Thirdly, the revolt may have precipitated changes in the attitude of the Sultan towards membership of the proposed federation of Malaysia. Whilst in some respects events strengthened the argument that membership would provide greater security, the revolt may also have sharpened pride in national sovereignty.

Through early 1963 negotiations between the Borneo states, the British and the Malaysian Prime Minister, Tunku Abdul Rahman, continued. The Cobbold Commission which visited North Borneo and Sarawak reported a generally favourable attitude towards federation (Andaya and Andaya, 1982, 272–4; Tarling, 1993, 199–203) but the attitude of Brunei fluctuated. Two issues appeared paramount. First, the status of the Sultan of Brunei in the rotating kingship proposed for Malaysia (the hereditary Sultans of Malaysia were to hold the position of Supreme Agong on a 5-year rotating basis) was problematic because, as the newest member, the Sultan of Brunei would be at the bottom in order of precedence (Leake, 1990, 55). Second, and perhaps more significant, was the fear that much of Brunei's oil wealth (and the suggestion that new off-shore deposits were being discovered gave added credence to this view) would be swallowed up by the Malaysian Treasury. In the end, the Sultan did not sign the treaty establishing the Federation. Neighbouring North Borneo (renamed Sabah) and Sarawak became founder members of the Federation of Malaysia in 1963; Brunei remained outside, prefiguring its eventual emergence as an independent sovereign state.

The 1960s and 1970s were periods of major economic and social change in the country. High rates of population increase with continued migration into the urban centres of Bandar Seri Begawan (the name given to Brunei Town in 1967), Seria and Kuala Belait, the expansion of development expenditure, and the increased revenues from the oil price rises of the 1970 meant major changes in the nature of Brunei society in the years immediately preceding independence. The population of Brunei grew from around 83,000 in 1960 to 192,832 in 1981 with Brunei-Malays comprising around 70 per cent of that total. The two major population centres of the state, Bandar Seri Begawan and the oilfield towns of Seria and Kuala Belait, continued to attract migrants from both rural areas, and, increasingly, from neighbouring countries, seeking work in the oil or construction sectors. As agriculture in the economy languished, new employment opportunities opened up, especially in the burgeoning public sector. Public sector employment doubled from 1960 to 1970 and more than doubled again to 1980 as government welfare programmes in education and health expanded.

Infrastructural programmes were of major significance in these two decades. The upgrading of both road communications (most notably the coast road) as well as telecommunications, were all signalled in the second and third development plans of this period. Other major projects embarked on by national planners included the establishment of a colour television broadcasting service, and the creation of Royal Brunei Airlines in 1975 as the national airline. Large scale public construction projects included many of the buildings in downtown Bandar Seri Begawan. Around the spectacular Omar Ali Saiffudin Mosque, completed in 1958, such buildings as the Treasury, Religious Affairs Department and Dewan Bahasa testify to the pace of construction in these years. School construction, the building of major hospitals in Kuala Belait and Bandar Seri Begawan moved on apace, especially as the increased oil revenues of the 1970s and early 1980s fed through to the Treasury.

The population itself was undoubtedly better-fed, better educated and better provided with material goods than ever before. As Table 2.4 indicates, indices such as the number of motor vehicles, the number of pilgrims making the *haj* pilgrimage, or the numbers of colour televisions all point to an increasingly prosperous society. It should be noted, though, that within that society there were considerable disparities in income and in levels of well-being. As one study of Kampong Ayer has

30   *Oil, Economic Development and Diversification*

Table 2.4   Material progress, 1970–90

	1970	1978	1988	1990
Motor vehicles	14 156	43 844	110 747	126 588
Airport departures	43 091	157 767	207 200	243 600
Televisions	—	23 123	58 500	67 000
Domestic electricity	43.41mkw	167.75	489.37	533.54

Source: Brunei Statistical Yearbooks.

noted (Cleary and Kam, 1992) the gap between rich and poor remained marked and was manifest both in terms of individual household incomes and differences between one kampong and another. As the country approached independence it did so with a budgetary surplus, sizeable investments, a rapidly modernising society and an increasingly open, more self-confident attitude to its neighbours.

2.6   AN INDEPENDENT NATION STATE

On January 1 1984 Brunei became an independent nation state, freed from any ties with Britain, and, henceforth, a sovereign state and member of the United Nations. Almost one hundred years of British influence, from the Protectorate declaration of 1888, was thus ended. Much of the impetus for independence had come from Britain, anxious to be rid both of accusations of colonialism and the costs of the self-government arrangements. On January 7 1979 a Treaty of Friendship and Cooperation was signed with Britain laying down a timetable for independence some five years later.

The years preceding independence were marked by a series of changes in Brunei. Construction projects such as the new National Stadium and the huge Istana Nurul Iman (Sultan's Palace) were undertaken, in part at least, as a demonstration of national pride. With foreign policy now in the hands of the state, diplomats strengthened the links with ASEAN nations — Malaysia, the Philippines, Thailand, Indonesia and Singapore — in readiness for the future framework of the new nation's policy. As Chapter 6 suggests, membership of ASEAN has given Brunei a much-enhanced role in the foreign policies of Southeast Asia.

The transition to independence did not go altogether smoothly. There were tensions over defence issues. The Sultan wanted to maintain a sizeable Ghurka force in the country after independence and, in return for paying for the upkeep of the force, sought some control over these units. The British government was adamant that this could not be conceded for fear that a British force might be used to suppress internal dissent in an independent nation. Eventually, in late-1983, an agreement was signed with the Ghurkas remaining under British command under a five-year renewable agreement which remains in force in 1993. British army officers and technicians also serve in the country's own Royal Brunei Armed Forces, on secondment from their British Army units. The Sultan retains his own, privately-recruited and funded force of Ghurka troops for his personal protection.

There were also some difficulties over the financial management of the assets of Brunei. Traditionally the Crown Agents of the British Government had been responsible for managing the investment portfolios of Brunei and, in 1983, it was estimated that Brunei funds represented some 90 per cent of the investment funds managed by the Crown Agents. In July 1983, at a time of rumbling discontent over the Ghurka question, the bulk of those foreign exchange holdings were transferred from the Crown Agents to a group of American and Japanese companies. As Leake (1990, 62) suggests, 'although Brunei began diversifying management of its funds in 1978, the abruptness and size of the July 1983 move gave it strong political overtones'.

On independence, Brunei adopted a ministerial style of government with the Sultan in Council having the ultimate responsibility for policy (Figure 2.2). Ministers are nominated by the Sultan; at present (1993) the Sultan retains the post of Prime Minister and Minister of Defence whilst his younger brother, Prince Muda Haji Jefri, retains the post of Minister of Finance. Another brother, Prince Muda Haji Mohamed is Minister of Foreign Affairs. The key posts in government are thus retained within the Royal Family with the Sultan himself retaining control of the Prime Minister's Office with its key sub-departments such as the Petroleum Unit, responsible for all aspects of royalties, taxes and conservation, the Council of Ministers and the Anti-Corruption Bureau. Mention should also be made of the use of the Royal *titah* to bring about particular administrative or ministerial reforms. On special occasions — National Day, for example, or at the end of the fasting period, the Sultan may use a speech to encourage particular shifts in attitudes. Whilst religious exhortations are perhaps more common, 'the *titah* has been used to ... prod the public service into a constant search for improvement of systems, processes and attitudes '(Wijeweera, 1992, 192).

Since independence, Brunei has modernised at a rapid and, to some political observers, alarming pace. Consumption of consumer durables has increased apace: Brunei now has one of the highest car ownership rates in the world and Bandar Seri Begawan, once a rather sleepy, river-bound town, snarls up with traffic like any other city. With the expansion of public housing projects, the city has expanded markedly in the last decade. The development of the new airport, and the concentration

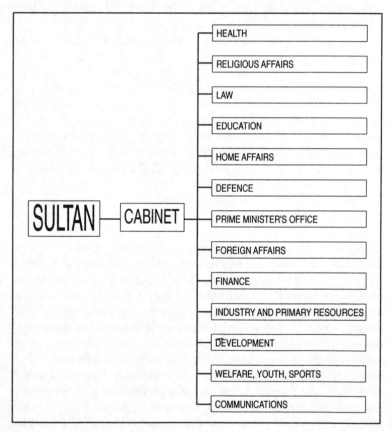

Figure 2.2   Structure of ministerial government

of government offices on the old airport site, has meant a continued expansion in public sector employment. A new University was established in 1985 and is due to move to a large site on the outskirts of the city in 1994. The expansion of the Institute of Technology, and the construction of a major Islamic School near Tutong exemplify the expansion of educational provision in the state. Considerable numbers of Bruneians are still sent abroad (primarily to the UK but also to Australia, New Zealand and Malaysia) for training in subjects which are not available in Brunei. The 25th Anniversary of the Accession of the Sultan, celebrated in October 1992 was marked by a further rash of public construction projects, most notably the new gold-domed mosque at Gadong, near the capital.

Alongside this continued expansion in consumption, in public sector projects and, in general, prosperity since independence has come an attempt to fashion a coherent ideological framework within which to situate the monarchy. The concept of Melayu Islam Beraja (Malay Islamic Monarchy) which emerged as part of the 1959 Constitution, has now taken a much greater role in the nation as a central plank in the post-independence polity of the state. As Mary-Ann Weaver recently noted (Weaver, 1991), MIB has been used to try to ensure that greater material prosperity and greater openness to the outside world (reflected, for example, in greater overseas travel) does not compromise the pre-eminent position of the Sultan and the Royal Family. MIB is a compulsory part of education programmes: all students at the University must take, and pass, MIB before proceeding with their degree programmes. An often-clumsy form of censorship of newspapers and journals seek to reinforce the MIB ideology and at least slow down those aspects of 'westernisation' deemed 'unsuited' to Brunei.

The decade or so since independence has thus been marked by a range of interesting social, economic and political developments. Material progress is self-evident in the country and this has been accompanied by greater access to education and a greater openness to the outside world. Politically Brunei is a stable member of ASEAN. Its political system is not modelled on western democracies and the emergence of an MIB philosophy has been viewed as an attempt to seek a political structure in the nation which will take account of the importance of the Monarchy and of Islam. The success or failure of this attempt will remain one of the more interesting aspects of Brunei's development into the twenty-first century. There can be little doubt that economic factors will continue to play a central part in the evolution of Bruneian society: the nature, meaning and pace of development are key issues that need to be examined both in terms of the ideologies of development strategy and the mechanics of development plans themselves. It is to these issues that the following chapters turn.

3 The Oil and Gas Industry

With the discovery of commercially viable quantities of oil in 1929, the economy of Brunei became closely linked to the global oil market and to external sources for the exploration, processing and disposal of its chief revenue earner. In the early 1990s, Brunei was the third largest producer of oil and natural gas in Southeast Asia after Indonesia and Malaysia; the country is ranked fourteenth in world production of oil and fourth in production of natural gas. This chapter outlines the development of the industry, patterns of production and the frameworks governing production, pricing and royalty arrangements. A final section considers the nature and extent of linkages between the hydrocarbon sector and the national economy.

3.1 EXPLORATION, DEVELOPMENT AND CONCESSION AREAS

Interest in the oil resources of Brunei began in the late nineteenth-century. With a steadily increasing rate of exploration in neighbouring Sarawak (resulting in the discovery of the Miri field in 1911, just across the Brunei-Sarawak border), and in Dutch Kalimantan (where the Balik-papan field came onstream at the turn of the century), it is not suprising that prospectors showed an interest in Brunei. The first exploratory wells were sunk in 1899 near Brunei Town and the Jerudong and Labi areas were also prospected; 'long before this', notes Harper (1975, 1),'oil prospectors had been travelling up and down north west Borneo investigating the numerous seepages in the area'. The wells, however, failed to yield commercial quantities of oil. Further wells were sunk after the discovery of the Miri field and there was a flurry of prospecting activity between 1911 and 1916.

From the outset, the British administration kept a tight control on the pattern of prospecting and exploration in the territory. The 1908 Brunei Mining Enactment distinguished between 'prospecting' and 'mining' leases. For the latter, a British character clause operated. At least 60 per cent of the subscribed capital of potential mining companies had to be held by British subjects, the majority of directors were to be British and

the company had to be registered in Britain. The application of the regulations was, however, less strict than the letter implied: as one Whitehall
official noted, 'Brunei was not quite like other places: its main need was
capital and, for my part, I didn't mind where the capital came from so
long as it came' (quoted in Horton, 1985, 260).

Between 1909 and the first exports of oil from the Seria field in 1931,
a number of foreign companies operated in Brunei. Figure 3.1 indicates
the most important ones. It highlights the close and early involvement of
Shell, who already held major interests in both the Miri and Balikpapan
fields on Borneo. In Brunei a Singapore-based company (Shanghai-
Langkat), a Dutch subsidary of the American company Standard Oil and
a Japanese company (Kuhara) all prospected unsuccessfully in these
early years. The largest concession holder in this period was the British
Borneo Petroleum Syndicate. As a largely British company, with a
number of influential shareholders, it was favoured by the administration with the major prospecting and mining leases. Horton (1985, 261),
however, has argued that because the company was chronically under-
capitalised, it was unable to take full advantange of the political and
administrative patronage it enjoyed. Its directors sought a number of
alliances with richer companies.

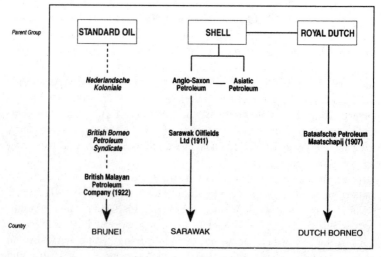

Figure 3.1   Companies involved in oil exploration in Borneo, 1907–22

Early negotiations with a Shell subsidary, the Anglo-Saxon Petroleum Company, active in Sarawak, failed in 1914 due to uncertainties over concession rights. After a series of abortive negotiations with other companies, an agreement was eventually signed in 1922. Together with the transfer of additional concession rights from another Shell company, the Asiatic Petroleum Company, the new company, the British Malayan Petroleum Company, had extensive prospecting and mining rights, and the necessary capital to take advantage of those rights. Under an agreement with the government, the new company agreed to a royalty of 2 shillings per ton (or 10 per cent in kind); in addition a royalty of 1 shilling per ton was to be paid to the British Borneo Petroleum Syndicate. The establishment of the new company gave Shell a near-monopoly of oil production in Borneo (Cleary and Eaton, 1992, 63–4).

It was to prove some considerable time before commercial quantities of oil were available. Prospecting continued in both the Jerudong and Seria districts. By mid-1930 it was clear that commercial quantities had been struck in the Seria district and in 1932 the first oil exports, some 176,000 tons of oil, were made. As Table 3.1 shows, exports rose steadily in value over the decade; by 1938 Brunei had become the largest single oil producer in the British Empire. Oil royalties fluctuated at around 12 per cent by value of all oil exported. By the late 1930s, oil exports accounted for around three-quarters of all state exports by value and the transformation of the economy of the country had begun.

Table 3.1   Oil exports, 1932–41

Year	Exports (S$ 000s)	As % all exports
1932	1,094	2%
1933	1,760	80%
1934	2,371	69%
1935	2,785	74%
1936	4,205	71%
1937	3,873	69%
1938	5,512	84%
1939	n.a.	n.a.
1940	7,515	78%
1941	4,388	66%

Source: Horton (1985), 281.

The physical transformation of the oil districts was slow and piece-meal. For most of the thirties, Miri in Sarawak was the operational head-quarters of the field, but gradually the oil infrastructure (oil storage and pumping facilities, gas compressor plant, housing) were developed and the oil town of Seria emerged from its swampy, crocodile-infested site. Kuala Belait expanded as an important centre for equipment and pur-chasing, and became a magnet for a growing oil workforce, much of it Chinese. It also became the District Office, replacing Kuala Balai, a small settlement up the Belait river. By 1940, oil exports had grown more than thirty-fold over the decade.

The Japanese Occupation in December 1941, and subsequent Allied invasion in June 1945, led to the large-scale destruction of the oil installations. They were disabled immediately prior to the Japanese arrival to prevent their use. Nonetheless, Harper (1975) suggests that the Japanese were able to extract considerable quantities of oil during the Occupation years perhaps amounting to one-half of pre-war levels. The departure of the Japanese again led to the destruction of much of the infrastructure, delaying efforts to bring oil onstream. Rehabilitation was fairly rapid, despite severe material shortages. Whilst the oilwell fires and extraction facilities were put in order quickly, the lack of facilities for storing and pumping crude oil from Seria to the main Lutong storage facilities in Sarawak was a problem. However, by 1948 120 potentially productive wells had been opened and actual output (well below potential output) stood at about 50,000 bpd, well above pre-war levels (Morrisson, 1951).

The Seria field was soon to reach maximum output; by the mid-1950s production was beginning to level off. The Jerudong field, coming onstream in 1955, produced disappointing yields and its deposits were exhausted by the late 1960s. In 1952 the first marine offshore oil plat-form was built, located in 9 metres of water about 1.5 km. from the coast, and by 1956 there were four such platforms operating, connected by cable car systems. In 1963 the country's first offshore oil and gas field, SouthWest Ampa, was discovered. Two years later production came onstream. The timing was fortuitous since onshore production from Seria was tailing off rapidly. In 1971 drilling for gas in the South-West Ampa field began with the gas being used to supply the Brunei LNG Sendiran Berhad plant at Lumut. By the mid-1980s there were some 40 drilling structures in the field from which over 250 wells had been drilled. Half of those wells are currently producing.

The Fairley field is located directly north of South West Ampa. Development began in 1972. Gas is piped to the Lumut plant by a subsea line from the Fairley-4 complex via the South West Ampa field. Crude oil from Fairley is transported via a trunk line to South West Ampa where it is mixed with the Ampa crude before being brought ashore at the Seria Terminal. The Champion Field was discovered in 1970 and lies about 70 km. north-east of Seria. Drilling began in 1972 and some 230 wells have been drilled in the field. Production is being maintained at between 50,000 and 60,000 bpd, making optimum use of natural reservoir processes. The oil is transported by pipeline to Seria. Compressed gas, presently some 50 MMscf/d, is delivered to Brunei LNG via a line and is used as boiler fuel. In 1993, Brunei Shell ordered a sixth gas compressor plant for the Champion field at a cost of $185 m. This will permit an extra 10 000 bpd to be extracted (Economist Intelligence Unit, 1993) The Magpie field, located about 60 km. north-east of Seria, was discovered in 1975. The first drilling platform was installed in 1977 and production began in the same year. Production peaked at 30,000 bpd in 1979. Current production is between 20,000 and 24,000 bpd. In addition to these fields, a number of other areas are being developed. These include Gannet, Iron Duke, Punyit and Egret (Figure 3.2). Jasra-Elf has also made a number of promising finds in the Maharaja Lela 2 field which is likely to produce sizeable quantities of hydrocarbons from the mid-1990s.

In order to prolong the life of its hydrocarbon reserves, Brunei Shell has invested heavily in enhanced recovery methods in the Seria field with new seismic work. A major survey, begun in February 1985, covered Kuala Belait, Seria, the jungle areas of Labi and Ulu Belait and a number of shallow offshore zones. In combination with further exploratory work, and with the use of high technology 3-dimensional computer methods, it is expected that further new or under-utilised resources will be discovered in the next decade.

Five companies currently hold concessions in Brunei: Brunei Shell, Jasra Jackson, the Sunray Borneo Oil Company, Superior Oil and Clark Brunei Oil and Woods Petroleum. Only Brunei Shell has carried out active exploration in recent years. A new joint venture company between Jasra and the French oil company Elf Aquitaine (known as Jasra-Elf) has however recently begun active exploration and, in 1990, was successful in striking hydrocarbons in a number of exploratory wells. Brunei Shell has historically held a virtual monopoly on

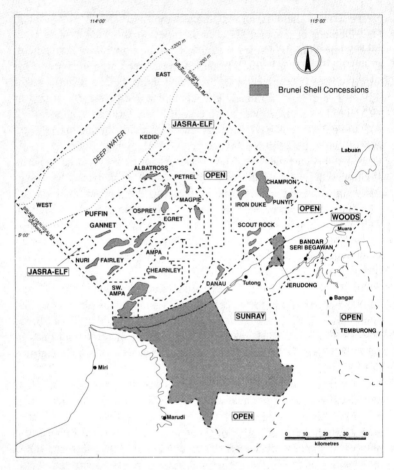

Figure 3.2   Oil and gas concession areas in 1989

exploration and production. It holds the largest concession areas in the
state. Prior to 1949, exploration was chiefly in the onshore areas around
Labi, Tutong, Jerudong and Seria. Its exploration acreage doubled after
1949 when areas between Seria and Labi, and Tutong and Bandar Seri
Begawan were licensed for exploration.

    In 1954 Brunei annexed its continental shelf and categorised as terri-
torial waters all offshore waters to a depth of 183 metres. With the passing of the Petroleum Mining Enactment in 1963, Brunei Shell

surrendered a number of its older, less productive concessions in exchange for new concessions; some 4,000 sq km were on the continental shelf, a further 680 sq km were in the Seria field. The company was granted a further offshore concession of 3,735 sq km in 1968 with parts of this concession extending beyond the continental shelf. A further 316 sq km were obtained in onshore areas and, in 1976, an additional 298 sq km near Labi was taken. Half of the offshore area granted in the 1963 concessions had been returned in 1976; the concession for the remaining offshore areas expires in 2003. Under the terms of the 1968 concession agreement, half of those concessions expired in 1980 with the remainder due for return in 2007. At the beginning of 1981, Brunei Shell was granted a third offshore concession area of some 3,530 sq km. The company is by far the largest concession holder with 10,107 sq km of territory, 73 per cent of which is offshore.

The exploration activity of most of the other companies has been concentrated, until recently, in the onshore areas. In 1964 Clark Brunei Oil and Refining Corporation took up a concession of 1968 sq km in the Tutong district, later joining with Sunray Borneo Oil Company and Superior Oil (B) Ltd. Additional concessions were granted to this group in 1985. A group comprising the Ashland Oil Company, Penzoil and Woods Petroleum were granted concessions in 1968, completing onshore and offshore seismic surveys in 1969 and 1970. In 1976 the consortium relinquished two concessions in the Belait district and part of their Temburong concession. They retain some 1,554 sq km of onshore concession, operating only 487 sq km of offshore areas. Jasra-Elf was granted 3,134 sq km of offshore concession (largely made up of concessions relinquished by Brunei Shell in 1976 and 1980) in 1982 (Gill, 1980). It struck commercial quantities of oil and gas in 1990 and seems likely to be the first company to break the Brunei Shell monopoly on production and export of hydrocarbons. Jasra-Elf nonetheless plans using Brunei Shell storage and processing facilities on a lease basis; at present, the set-up costs of establishing its own infrastructure cannot be commercially justified.

3.2 PATTERNS OF OIL AND GAS PRODUCTION

Table 3.2 indicates the patterns of production of oil and gas between 1950 and 1990. As was noted in Chapter 2, production rose steadily

Table 3.2   Oil and natural gas production, 1950–90

Year	Crude oil (barrels)	Natural gas (000 cu.m)
1950	30,543,476	753,655
1955	38,879,361	1,177,071
1959	39,565,614	1,782,847
1965	28,850,880	—
1970	49,001,050	—
1975	64,335,410	7,686,000
1980	81,890,760	10,092,000
1985	53,860,840	8,494,000
1990	52,189,600	8,977,000

Source: Brunei Darussalam Yearbooks.

through the 1930s; the Japanese Occupation and subsequent Allied recapture of the fields produced major disruptions in production but output recovered remarkably quickly given the major infrastructural and material difficulties prevailing in the field. By the late 1940s, production was back at pre-war levels and the onshore Seria field reached peak production in 1956 at 115,000 bpd.

After 1956 production in the Seria field began to tail off in spite of a sizeable increase in drillings to over 600. A large number of drillings were needed because of the geological conditions, with folding dividing the field into numerous discrete blocks. New production technologies and better recovery methods have meant that the Seria field continues to produce albeit at a rather low level with an average yield per well of around 120 bpd in the late 1980s compared with a Middle Eastern average of about 6,000 bpd. The Seria output, has a low sulphur content and produces both light and heavy petroleum. The yields in the other onshore field, Jerudong, have been poor. Production was discontinued in the 1960s and total production from the field amounted to only 90,000 tons.

The discovery and development of the South West Ampa field brought about marked increases in oil production and by the end of the 1960s, the production peak of 1957 had been overtaken. Of the total output of about 140,000 bpd in 1969, some 76,000 came from the new field. By the late 1970s the field had produced a total of almost 50 million tons of oil. Furthermore, its development had a profound effect on the technologies used in Brunei; large drilling platforms were required and new technologies were imported by Brunei Shell. By the early 1980s there were about 120 wells operating in the field. Two further off-shore fields have been developed since the early 1970s. The Champion field came onstream in 1972 with an initial capacity of about 18,000 bpd. Production has risen steadily to about 50,000 bpd from 200 wells in 1983 but has steadied since then. The third field, Magpie, began pro-duction in 1978, and produces almost exclusively natural gas.

The discovery and development of the new offshore fields permitted major increases in oil production in the state. From levels of around 140,000 bpd in 1970, production soared during the first oil crisis to about 225,000 bpd in 1974. By 1979 production had reached in excess of 250,000 bpd of which about 80 per cent came from offshore produc-tion. Production in the early 1980s fell to an average of about 160,000 bpd reflecting both a fall in demand and a conservation policy instituted by government, pegging production from 1987 to about 150,000 bpd. The National Petroleum Depletion Policy instituted in 1981 places tight limits on production in order to conserve existing oil reserves. The number of wells operative has however continued to increase from 421 in 1974 to 721 in 1984. By 1989, however, they had fallen to 558. Aver-age production per well has fallen steadily, reflecting the increased difficulties inherent in the fields; in 1974 average production per active well was around 22,400 tons; by 1984 it had fallen to 10,540 tons (Energy Information Administration, 1984).

Estimates of the production capacity of Brunei's fields suggest an annual capacity of about 210,000 bpd. 98 per cent of this is exported; the remainder is refined locally and sold for domestic consumption. The Gulf War saw an upsurge in production triggerred by the absence of exports from Kuwait and Iraq. Brunei produced an additional 0.7 mil-lion barrels of oil in the last quarter of 1990, pushing output a little above the planned annual target. A number of additional liquified natu-ral gas cargoes were also sold to Japan. In view of the destruction of Kuwait's oil installations, and the ban imposed by the UN on Iraqi oil exports, it is likely that Bruneian production will continue at levels a little higher than those anticipated by the conservation programme. Pro-duction was 182,000 bpd in 1992; the 1993 figure is expected to be around 165,000.

In the early years of production, Brunei's oil was transported by pipeline to a tank in Kuala Belait from where it was taken by ship to Lutong, near Miri, where it was reloaded into deep sea vessels for export alongside oil produced by Shell from the Miri fields. By 1939 a pipeline and connecting road had been built between Kuala Belait and Miri to facilitate oil exports from Brunei. With the post- war reconstruction of the installations, two further pipelines were developed to cope with the increased production of the Brunei field. To increase storage capacity, three tanks were constructed at Seria in 1947 with individual capacities of about 40,000 barrels. During periods of peak production, oil was temporarily stored so that the pipeline capacity to Lutong could be used with maximum efficiency.

Rises in production eventually prompted the construction of a single buoy mooring facility at Seria in 1972 allowing for the direct shipping of oil, by-passing the Lutong facilities. The oil terminal at Seria was extended with the construction of five new tanks, each with a capacity of 310,000 barrels, connected with the mooring buoy by a 10 km submarine pipeline. Initially only light oils and the offshore oils were shipped here; heavy oil and oil products continued to be exported via Lutong. With the rises in production in the early 1970s, the storage capacity of the tanks in Seria were soon stretched. In 1977 a second mooring facility was built at Seria together with the construction of additional, emergency storage facilities. The nine tanks now available at Seria can store about two weeks of oil production.

3.3   NATURAL GAS PRODUCTION

Brunei is the world's fourth largest producer of natural gas after Indonesia, Malaysia and Algeria and has been a pioneer in the industry following Algeria's lead in developing LNG facilities for the sale of gas on a long-contract basis (Banks, 1987, 50). Gas production in Brunei began with the discovery and development of the South West Ampa field and has been consolidated by gas from the Fairley and Champion fields. The gas industry has developed rapidly in Brunei and has spawned both new technologies and new company structures within Brunei Shell. Brunei LNG, Brunei Coldgas and Brunei Shell Tankers have been created in order to facilitate gas production and export. Their structure is described later.

When the South West Ampa field was found to contain large quantities of natural gas, there were a limited number of options available for Brunei Shell. The scope for exporting to local markets was limited; demand in Brunei was small. The best market, Japan, could hardly be tapped given the costs of a pipeline of over 4,000 km. The use of gas liquefaction techniques remained a possibility. The technology had developed in the 1950s with the first large-scale gas liquefaction plant being built at Arzew, Algeria in 1964. The Brunei liquefaction plant was to have about 5 times the capacity of the Arzew plant and required major capital investment in plant and technology.

The LNG plant at Lumut, about 30 km east of Seria, was opened in 1973 and, at the time, was the largest plant of its kind in the world. It has the capacity to produce about 6 million tons of liquid gas per year. An electricity generating plant with a 40 megawatt capacity was also built to run the cooling aggregates. The Badas Water Plant was constructed nearby to supply water to the facility as well as to the towns of Kuala Belait and Seria. An additional water purification plant was built at Lumut. A four and a half km jetty was built from the Lumut plant to allow access to deep water for the LNG tankers used to transport the liquid gas to the Japanese market. Natural gas to the Lumut plant comes by pipeline from three fields — South West Ampa, Fairley and Champion — respectively 18, 35 and 70 km from the plant. A new gas field, Champion West, will come onstream in 1994.

Average daily production of gas in the late 1980s stood at just over 1,000 million standard cubic feet of which about 80 per cent was exported. Total gross production rose from 4,500 million cubic metres in 1972 to about three times that figure in the late-1980s. All the exports go to three public utility companies in Japan — Tokyo Gas, Tokyo Electric and Osaka Gas. Brunei was a pioneer of the LNG trade in the ASEAN region. In 1968, when plans were developing to build the Lumut plant, it signed an agreement with the three companies named above to deliver LNG by tanker under a twenty-year contract. In Japan, terminals at Negishi, Sodegaura and Senboku were built to receive the LNG tankers which were leased and later owned by Brunei Shell Tankers.

In 1987 a co-generation plant was opened at Lumut to generate electricity for domestic and industrial purposes in Brunei. Completed at a cost of $310 million it was a joint venture between Brunei Shell Petroleum, the Department of Electrical Services and Brunei LNG. Its aim was to meet increased power demands which the existing, rather ageing generators in Seria could not cope with. The plant supplies more than 20 per cent of Brunei LNG's steam requirements. A new gas compression plant completed in Seria also allows for the more efficient use of gas produced from the Seria field.

Given the uncertainty over prices and declining reserves, efforts have been made to contain the operating costs of the Lumut plant. Total operating expenditure fell from $927 million in 1986 to $841 million in 1987. However, major projects have continued as the renewal of the 20-year agreement governing exports came close to expiry. The Gannet field, 55 km. off Seria, was inaugurated in July 1988, producing 150 million cubic feet of gas per day (about 10 per cent of the total) and Champion West will provide additional gas. Brunei Shell have also announced projects to upgrade production facilities in the Champion field as a whole. Onshore a major refurbishment of the Lumut plant was undertaken in 1991–2 in preparation for the new 20-year supply contract, which was signed in March 1993. Under the terms of the contract, negotiated under more stringent conditions than the first (and with greater competition from other LNG producers), the number of tanker cargoes each year will rise from 152 to about 165. Overall LNG exports to Japan are expected to rise from 5.14 million tons a year under the old contract to 5.54 million tons under the new.

3.4   OPERATIONAL STRUCTURE AND LEGISLATION

From exploration to development and maturity, foreign companies have dominated the oil industry in Brunei. As elsewhere on Borneo, Shell has played the key role. The present company responsible for most oil production in the state, Brunei Shell Petroleum Company Limited, was formed as a locally-registered company in 1957. It was the first company to be incorporated under the Brunei Companies Enactment of January 1 1957 and was fully owned by the Shell Group. The new company took over all the personnel, assets and contracts of the old, British Malayan Petroleum Company which had previously dominated production. The company title was chosen to emphasise the close and long-standing connections between the state and the operations of the Royal Dutch/Shell group of companies.

The relationship between transnational oil companies and their host state has often been complex and controversial, particularly with the changed economic and political environment of the 1970s. Countries in the region adopted different strategies to ensure greater access to the financial benefits of oil production. Thus neighbouring Indonesia and Malaysia have developed a range of measures such as production-sharing contracts and increased state control through national companies (e.g. Pertamina in Indonesia; Petronas in Malaysia) to secure good returns on state assets (Cleary and Eaton, 1992, 214–16). Whilst Brunei did not remain unaffected by the more volatile environment of the 1960s and 1970s, its strategy for maintaining control over oil production was rather less radical than elsewhere. Increased participation in the industry has been sought within the framework of the traditional concession system rather than through nationalisation or production-sharing contracts.

The Petroleum Mining Act (Laws of Brunei, Revisions of 1984) is the basic legislative act governing the operation of the industry in both onshore and offshore areas of the state. The Act lays down a number of conditions for the granting of concessions and their operation. These include clauses relating to the length of the concession agreement, surrender conditions, fixed payments and royalty and taxation conditions. In general concessions are granted for 30 years with the possibility of renewal for a further 30 year period. Relinquishing of concessions is phased in the legislation: 50 per cent are to be relinquished after 8 years for onshore and 10 years for offshore concessions. An additional 25 per cent of the concession has to be relinquished after 15 years for onshore and 17 years for offshore areas. Work expenditure obligations are also specified. Minimum expenditure of specified amounts are required according to acreage during the first 3 years for onshore and 5 years for offshore concessions. Fixed annual payments are required in subsequent years, such payments being deductible from royalties. Companies also gain exclusive rights over their operations and discoveries in exchange for these conditions. Subject to certain limitations, they may also use other resources as and when required for their operations (e.g. they may enter adjacent lands, erect offices, use water, etc.).

Royalty payments differ for onshore and offshore fields. For the former a flat royalty (in cash or kind) equivalent to 12.5 per cent is payable. For offshore fields, the royalty is 10 per cent on fields between 3 and 10 nautical miles offshore; 8 per cent for those more than 10 nautical miles offshore. Similar conditions apply to natural gas production. Amendments made to the Petroleum Mining Act have altered the tax treatment of royalties. Under the old arrangement, royalties were not regarded as a cost for tax purposes but were credited against company taxes payable. Since 1982, royalties have been treated as a cost when assessing taxable income which is not offset against tax payable; in other words, it was expensed (Hamzah, 1992, 161). This arrangement served to increase the amount paid as tax to the Brunei government by about 50 per cent of royalty levels. In addition the price at which oil was valued for taxation purposes was no longer the realised price, but a posted price related to crude oil prices in the Gulf. Finally, the model agreements lay down strict conditions regarding the abandonment of wells, waste disposal, restoration of mined land and accounting procedures. The legislation also clarifies government rights to participation in the company. If exploitable rights are discovered, the government has the right to purchase a 50 per cent share in the development and exploitation of the field.

In 1973, in a move which reflected the desire for greater participation in the oil and gas industry, the government bought a 25 per cent share in Brunei Shell Petroleum. The move coincided with the first oil price hike and brought substantial increases in both company profits and government royalties and receipts. A further change in 1985 increased overall government participation in the company to 50 per cent with the remaining shares being held by the Royal Dutch/Shell group. The contemporary structure of Brunei Shell is indicated in Figure 3.3. It operates as a

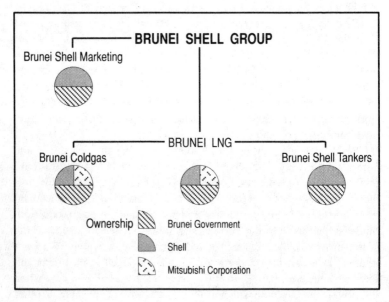

Figure 3.3   Company structure of Brunei Shell in 1990

group of five companies. Brunei Shell Petroleum is the main company responsible for the exploration and production of oil and LNG.

Brunei Shell Marketing was established in 1974 in order to sell oil and gas products within the state. The company is jointly owned by the government and Shell with its headquarters in Bandar Seri Begawan. The company sells a range of products — gasolines, aviation fuel, diesel oil, lubricants, butane gas in cylinders and some chemical products such as insecticides and detergents. It has a monopoly on petroleum sales in the state and has thus recorded large increases in sales, as the number of motor vehicles in Brunei increases. There are 21 petrol stations in the country, all supplied by Brunei Shell Marketing. Prices are low by international standards with the government determining overall levels. High octane petrol is imported from Singapore, as is diesel, and is stored in tanks at the port of Muara. The Muara depot also supplies oil and petrol to riverine stations in the Brunei River and Temburong River. Asphalt is also imported from Singapore and stored adjacent to the fuel tanks at Muara. Aviation fuels are also supplied by Brunei Shell Marketing for the international airport at Bandar Seri Begawan and fuels for running the main electricity generating plant at Gadong, near the capital, are supplied by the company.

The other three companies — Brunei Liquified Natural Gas (BLNG), Brunei Coldgas (BCG) and Brunei Shell Tankers were all formed to cater for the LNG trade with Japan. Brunei LNG was formed in 1969 after a joint venture agreement between the three partners — the government, Shell Petroleum and the Mitsubishi Corporation. Initially Shell and Mitsubishi had 45 per cent of the shares each; the government share was later increased to 50 per cent. Brunei LNG was established to build and operate the Lumut LNG plant, completed in 1973, for exporting LNG to Japan. The multinational character of Brunei LNG is reflected in the technology used to build the Lumut plant. Brunei Shell, the American company, Air Products and Chemicals Inc. and a joint Shell Mitsubishi company, Nippon LNG KK were all closely involved in design, purchasing and construction. As noted earlier, the plant required a 4.5 km. jetty with two stainless steel pipelines to transport the gas to the tankers, as well as a special water purification plant. Materials were imported via a specially built cargo jetty. The plant cost some $600 million. It is a capital intensive operation employing only some 100 people excluding the special Ghurka security personnel employed on site.

The LNG produced by Brunei LNG is marketed by a fourth company, Brunei Coldgas which was established in 1977. Half of the shares are government owned, the remainder are divided equally between Shell and Mitsubishi. Finally, the fifth arm of the company, Brunei Shell Tankers, is responsible for transporting LNG to the Japanese consumers and for ensuring the efficient synchronisation of tanker scheduling and LNG production. When LNG shipments began, the seven tankers used on the 9,000 kilometre loop voyage to Japan were leased from Shell Tankers (UK). In December 1986 a new company, Brunei Shell Tankers, was formed and the seven tankers leased from Shell Tankers (UK) were bought by the company. The government and Shell Group have equal shares in the company. All the tankers are registered in Brunei and fly the Brunei flag. Each can transport some 75,000 cubic metres of LNG and a tanker makes a delivery in Japan about every 60 hours. About 5 million tons of LNG were delivered annually by the fleet in the early 1990s.

In addition to government control exercised through board membership of Brunei Shell companies, the Petroleum Unit, part of the Prime Minister's Office, plays a key role in determining general production, conservation and pricing policies. A new government grouping, the Brunei Oil and Gas Authority, was established in early-1993 under the chairmanship of the Minister of Finance, Jefri Bolkiah. The new body is likely to assume responsibility for planning production levels and the granting of concession rights and will almost certainly replace some of the functions of the Petroleum Unit.

3.5   OIL PRICING POLICIES

Given the high dependence of Brunei's economy on oil, pricing policies are of critical importance. Brunei, as a small producer, can exert relatively little control over global oil prices. It is not a member of OPEC and any policies of restraint it might advocate would have no impact on global oil production. Its agreements with the main producer, Brunei Shell, can however have some impact on price and production. In the pre-war period prices and production were governed almost entirely by external companies with Royal Dutch Shell, the parent company of the British Malayan Petroleum Company, being the main broker of production and pricing.

In the postwar period, the political and economic environment of oil production changed markedly. A number of countries took the lead in securing profit-sharing agreements with the major multinationals which gave host countries some say in production and pricing; nationalisation provided an alternative scenario. As noted above, the policies of Brunei were fairly conservative in this respect with production-sharing and profit-sharing agreements being the preferred means of negotiating with the main producer. The key event in influencing global prices, in which Brunei played no part, was the formation of OPEC in September 1960. Besides influencing production levels with the aim of raising prices, OPEC spearheaded changes in methods of calculating company profits by expensing royalties. As has been suggested this had the effect of raising state revenues from oil taxes in Brunei.

The 1967 Arab-Israeli conflict, coupled with rapid increases in oil consumption as economic growth spiralled in the west, stimulated shifts in attitudes ' amongst the key OPEC producers which ultimately benefited Brunei. In particular, OPEC introduced the principle of price-setting through negotiation between producing states and companies rather than through unilateral company action. The key instrument, that of controlling production levels, was soon widely employed by states anxious to secure the best possible relationhip between fiscal needs and conservation policies. In Brunei these shifts were reflected in the establishment of profit sharing agreements from the early 1970s as Brunei Shell Petroleum was progressively restructured to increase government share capital.

Government control of Brunei Shell is reflected in number of ways. It is represented on the Board of Directors of all the constituent Brunei Shell companies. As noted above, the Petroleum Unit and the Brunei Oil and Gas Authority serve to maintain a degree of government control. The format of concession agreements also gives the state a share in decision-making as well as the right to profit-sharing in any new discoveries should it wish to exercise that right. The oil price hikes of 1973 led to major direct benefits to the state. Indirect benefits included the long term LNG contract with Japan which chose Brunei as a stable and secure regional LNG supplier at a time of major uncertainties over gas production in the Gulf. Further oil price rises in 1979 had additional major impacts on company profits and government revenue. Trends on prices in the 1980s were varied; the outlook for the 1990s is likely to continue to be unsettled with increasingly difficult trading conditions for producers although, regionally, demand for oil continues to be buoyant in the Asia-Pacific market (Shankar, Sharma and Tan, 1991, 3).

As a small world producer, the price for Brunei's oil follows closely international trends; LNG prices have fluctuated in a similar fashion. Traditionally there are three different notional prices for crude oil — transfer price, market price and the posted price. Much of the exploration, production, processing and marketing of hydrocarbons is still controlled by the major oil companies and their affiliates. The price at which crude oil is invoiced from producing to refining affiliates is known as the transfer price; its level reflects in large part the need to maximise company consolidated profits. A proportion of crude output may be sold on the open market. The price at which such transactions occur is known as the market price or spot market price. These may be distorted by a range of factors including freight concessions, tied loans or concessionary rates, buy-back committments or generous delivery terms.

The posted price is usually defined as the 'public offering price by the seller freight on board at port of origin'. Prior to the early 1970s, the posted price often bore little relationship to wider conditions of supply and demand and, in general, only minimal quantities of oil were sold at posted prices. Frequently the posted price was simply an internal price used by producing affiliates to bill refining affiliates for the supply of crude. For oil-producing companies, the posted price serves as a yardstick with which to determine oil revenues and tax liabilities; posted prices thus vary depending on the sulphur content of the oil, specific gravity and distance from the major market.

In general Brunei's crude oil prices have followed those of the OPEC producers. As Table 3.3 indicates, these have varied dramatically over the last two decades reflecting both changing political climates and changing energy demands from the major global economies. The major rises of 1973 and 1979 have been juxtaposed with marked falls at other times. Brunei normally sells its oil under long term contracts. This pattern has, however, altered in recent years. From the late 1970s, as spot prices for crude oil rose, a newly established subsidary company under Royal control bought between 20,000 and 40 000 bpd of crude from Brunei Shell Petroleum and marketed it on its own account on the spot market (Gill, 1980). This move, whilst exposing oil to greater price fluctuations, potentially increased revenues by selling on the volatile spot market.

Table 3.3   Average world oil prices, 1960–92

Year	Price (US$/b)
1960	1.80
1965	1.80
1970	1.85
1975	11.25
1980	40.00
1985	27.00
1990	18.91
1992	16.22

Since 1985 Brunei Shell Petroleum has shifted to more flexible marketing systems for its product. In general higher quantities are now sold on the spot market and there has been a corresponding reduction in long term contracts. Furthermore, new contracts incorporate more flexible pricing systems. The move reflected global pricing trends: in general those producers prepared to be more flexible by selling on the spot market (usually at prices lower than contract market prices) gained increased sales. That shift has largely reflected the surpluses in oil production for much of the 1980s with much lower prices evident. The changed world market has also induced changes in the traditional trading systems. Instead of making all sales on a freight-on-board basis, Brunei Shell now increasingly charters tankers to deliver oil directly to consumers, a system which can result in lower costs and increased flexibility.

3.6   TRADING PATTERNS AND RESERVES

The bulk of Brunei's hydrocarbons are marketed overseas. Figure 3.4. indicates the approximate amounts marketed domestically in 1990, based on an average oil production of 150,000 bpd and gas production of 750 million cubic feet. Only small quantities enter the local market (some 4 per cent of oil and 8 per cent of LNG) through Brunei Shell Marketing or through the use of gas for electricity generation and domestic consumption. The remainder is marketed overseas. The pattern of markets has shifted somewhat in recent decades. The major customer remains Japan. In 1970 about two-thirds of Brunei's total oil exports went to Japan. Whilst that proportion has fallen since the early 1980s with the shift to sale on the spot market, Japan still absorbed about 25 per cent of the oil output in 1989 (Table 3.4).

A number of other countries in the region now absorb increasing quantities of oil. Prior to 1982, South Korea took virtually no oil from Brunei; by 1989 almost 25 per cent of crude was shipped to South Korea. Clearly the impact of the oil crises has led South Korea to favour regional producers rather than rely on deliveries from the Gulf. The drive for industrialisation in South Korea has also increased energy demands. Two other oil-deficient newly industrialised countries in the region, Singapore and Taiwan also take around 10 per cent of Brunei's oil output respectively. The ASEAN market is important to Brunei: ASEAN countries took almost 40 per cent of output in the late 1980s with Thailand in particular sourcing oil supplies from Brunei.

Exports of LNG go entirely to three customers in Japan — Tokyo Gas, Tokyo Electric and Osaka Gas. These supplies are delivered under the terms of the twenty-year contracts negotiated for 1973–93 and 1993–2013. Overall, Brunei supplies about 16 per cent of Japan's LNG requirements; at present, Indonesia and Malaysia supply greater quantities of LNG to the Japanese market than does Brunei. As a pioneer producer in 1972, Brunei was able to negotiate good contract terms with its

Table 3.4   Crude oil exports by country of destination (%), 1978–89

Year	Japan	S.Korea	Taiwan	S'pore	Thail.	Phil.	Other
1978	63.5	0	6.4	7.4	2.0	0.1	20.6
1979	61.6	0	6.1	8.2	2.2	2.2	19.7
1980	58.9	0	2.6	10.0	6.7	1.8	20.0
1981	46.9	0	0	12.0	5.7	5.4	30.0
1982	44.3	7.6	2.0	9.8	4.6	3.6	28.1
1983	47.2	13.5	4.9	9.2	8.3	3.1	13.8
1984	46.5	9.6	3.8	11.8	11.5	3.0	13.8
1985	34.3	12.9	6.5	14.3	19.5	0.9	11.6
1986	34.0	17.4	4.1	3.9	19.9	1.8	8.9
1987	35.4	8.1	4.9	0.6	23.9	6.6	0.5
1988	32.9	22.2	6.9	9.9	20.7	4.7	2.7
1989	25.4	25.1	7.2	7.4	21.8	5.4	7.7

Source: Brunei Darussalam Statistical Yearbooks.

Japanese customers; its negotiations over the second contract were more difficult given the greater competition from Malaysia, Indonesia and Australia. The fact that Brunei had been able to maintain an unbroken and trouble-free supply of LNG from 1972–92 was an important consideration.

Precise data on reserves is not accessible since it is regarded as confidential by both the government Petroleum Unit which oversees the industry, and the companies engaged in exploration and production. Data from 1983 (Energy Information Administration, 1984) estimated proven exploitable reserves at 753 million barrels with additional indicative reserves of 420 million barrels. Given these figures, a reserves/production ratio of about 13 years was suggested rising to 21 if indicative reserves were included. These estimates may be regarded as conservative given the new discoveries and improved recovery methods of the late-1980s. A 1990 survey (Oil and Gas Journal, 1991) upgraded potential exploitable reserves to about 1,375 million barrels with a new reserves/production ratio of some 26 years. Clearly the figures are subject to fluctuation as demand and price can change rapidly, government conservation policies can alter production levels and, most significantly, changing technologies alter productive reserves and recovery rates. Despite long production from both onshore and offshore fields in Brunei, both proven and probable reserves have continued to rise. With proven reserves likely to allow the maintenance of current production levels for at least twenty-five years, and given improved recovery rates in the key South West Ampa and Champion fields, the medium-term outlook for hydrocarbon production is reasonably secure.

Natural gas reserves were estimated at about 11.6 trillion cubic feet in 1989, with a reserve/production ratio of about 38 years. Developments in Champion West may suggest an upgrading of that ratio to almost 50 years. Current estimates suggest that about 36 per cent of Brunei's reserves have thus far been recovered. The scope for improving overall recovery rates for gas is probably more limited than in the case of petroleum. However, reserves are more than adequate to fulfill the conditions imposed by the new 20-year contract with Japan, to meet domestic consumption and to supply the industrial needs of Brunei Shell Petroleum well into the next decade. Whilst about 60 per cent of gas reserves were situated in the South West Ampa field, additional reserves are likely to be discovered as both Brunei Shell and Jasra-Elf continue active exploration.

3.7   HYDROCARBONS AND THE LOCAL ECONOMY

The production of hydrocarbons impacts on the Brunei economy in a variety of ways and some of the fiscal and development implications of the industry will be examined in Chapters 4 and 5. A brief synopsis of some of the key economic impacts will be given here.

Domestic consumption of hydrocarbons is catered for entirely by Brunei Shell. Since the construction of the refining facility at Seria in 1983, Brunei has been fully self-sufficient in basic petroleum fuels. The construction of the refinery was as much a political as an economic move; its relatively small size makes it largely uneconomic and, because of the small market in Brunei it often runs at below capacity. A small quantity of platformate is imported from Singapore to enable higher qualities of petroleum to be produced for the local market. There has been a massive growth in petroleum consumption in Brunei in the last two decades. Car ownership is widespread; the country has one of the highest per capita ownership rates in the world. The availability of interest-free car loans for public servants, coupled with high per capita incomes, has facilitated this growth. Average annual growth rates of 6 or 7 per cent in petroleum consumption have not been uncommon in the last decade. Substantial programmes of electrification have also increased consumption of gas for electricity generation. Butane gas supplies have also grown as kerosene is replaced as a cooking fuel. Whilst domestic consumption has grown apace, it still consumes only a small proportion of total production (Figure 3.4).

Perhaps the most obvious impact of hydrocarbons has been the fiscal one; whilst this is examined more fully in the following chapter, a few comments are appropriate here. Oil revenues accruing to the government come from royalties on oil produced, corporate taxation and profit-sharing arrangements. The nature of the national accounts makes it difficult to disentangle one from the other. Royalty payments have varied for a variety of reasons. First, the legislation has been altered on a number of occasions, notably in enactments in 1949, 1955, 1963 and 1969. Secondly, as production has altered and the balance between onshore and offshore production changed, royalty payments have varied. Thirdly, profit-sharing agreements have tended to lead to a reduction in royalty revenues in favour of the potentially higher returns from such schemes. Royalty rates are broadly comparable with those in the Middle East.

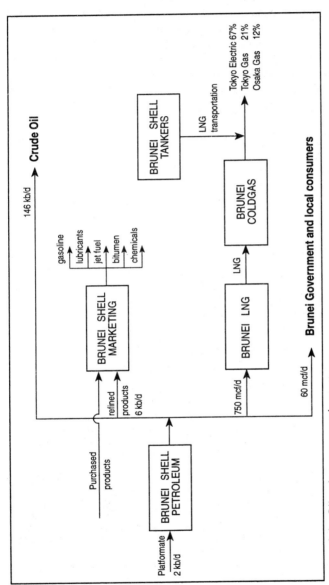

Figure 3.4 Oil and gas consumption patterns

Corporate taxes have been a more important source of revenue in recent years and they currently account for around 50 per cent of total oil revenues. Current tax rates on petroleum profits are 50 per cent (Hamzah, 1992, 135). Taxes on LNG profits were not levied during the first five years of production; since 1977 they have been fixed at 45 per cent.

Oil and natural gas remain by far the principal exports of the state. As Figure 3.5 shows, they have consistently accounted for well over 90 per cent of all exports by value since the mid-1970s. The fall in total export revenues from oil from the mid-1980s reflects both falling prices and the policy of conservation pursued by the Petroleum Unit with production being pegged at around 150,000 bpd, although in recent years that figure has been exceeded.

The hydrocarbon industry in Brunei exhibits many of the characteristics of an enclave economy. Technical, labour and capital linkages have

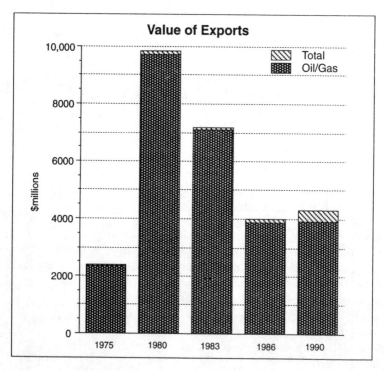

Figure 3.5   State exports by value, 1975–90

often been stronger with external countries and companies than with domestic structures. The industry is capital-intensive, relying heavily on imported skills and technology. Furthermore, the small size of the country has restricted the potential for major spin-offs such as petrochemicals to develop. Such enterprises would hardly be viable given the labour costs and infrastructural needs of any proposed projects. The proximity of a sophisticated petrochemical industry in Singapore further mitigates against such developments.

The direct impact of the hydrocarbon sector on employment patterns is relatively small due to the capital-intensive nature of the industry. Employment in this sector accounted for around 6 per cent of total employment in Brunei in 1990. The prospects for any sizeable increase in employment in this sector are limited. In absolute terms, the industry employs about 5,000 workers in total. Whilst there was a small increase in employment during the 1980s, this is most unlikely to alter in the next decade, although there may be opportunities for employment in Jasra-Elf if, as seems likely, its role in the industry expands. There have however been major improvements in the balance between citizens and expatriate workers in the major employer, Brunei Shell. There has been a concerted policy of increasing the employment of Brunei citizens in the company and reducing reliance on expatriates. The proportion of citizens working for the company grew from 37 per cent in 1980 to over 50 per cent in 1990, reflecting the committment to a programme of Bruneianisation. Whilst citizen employment still remains concentrated in the lower echelons of the industry, the expansion of training programmes suggests that this is likely to alter quite rapidly. The government and Brunei Shell have indicated strong commitments to this programme, especially since independence.

Indirect employment arising from the industry is much harder to estimate. Overall, the multiplier effects of the oil and gas industries tend to be low. Linkages with the production sector of the economy are weak; much of the technology and machinery continues to be imported with most sub-contracting work going to established overseas firms. A strong network of locally owned and staffed firms catering to the industry simply does not exist. Most of the sub-contracting firms engaged in offshore drilling in particular come from regional offices in Singapore. Whilst Brunei Shell Petroleum has its own shipyard facility in Kuala Belait, employing about 60 people, most of the more sophisticated equipment is imported directly from Europe or the United States.

Subcontracting firms provide most of the highly specialised technical services. Three large international companies are active in offshore drilling — Reading Bates, Sedoo and Aquadrill. McDermott, an international company specialising in oil pipeline construction has a subsidiary company in Brunei as does Reading Bates. Both employ around 200 people. Schlumberger specialises in the analysis of drilling reports and employs some 60 people locally. Most of the underwater installations are handled by an international company, Subsea Oil Services. Several other small companies work as subcontractors to Brunei Shell; most are American firms operating through subsidiaries based in Singapore with only a skeleton staff in Brunei.

The hydrocarbon industry in Brunei is confined to 'upstream' activities, that is, the production and processing of oil and gas. 'Downstream' activities have not developed, despite long term government plans to instigate such growth. Such industries might include a diverse range of products. The production of ethylene, fertilisers or refined lubricants typify such developments. Synthetics, notably PVC, might also be produced in the early stages of such downstream development. Thus far, no progress has been made on such developments.

The spin-offs for the service sector may be rather more significant. The retailing sector benefits from the employment and wages generated in the industry with the economies of Kuala Belait and Seria heavily dependent on the oil sector. Similarly demand for services is higher as a result of the industry. Rentals on housing for expatriate staff can produce income for the local economy although this is limited since much expatriate housing is provided directly by Brunei Shell.

The hydrocarbon industry has undoubtedly reshaped the geography of the state. The towns of Kuala Belait and Seria were both products of the industry. Seria, in particular, with its extensive areas of company housing, grid street pattern and network of 'nodding donkeys' interspersed in the town is set apart from the indigenous towns and villages elsewhere in the state. The hotels, restaurants and commerce in these towns cater almost exclusively to the oil and gas industry. But, as noted above, there has been little diversification; both towns depend very heavily on the industry and there are signs that as the industry reaches its capacity for employment some out-migration to the capital is taking place, raising significant long-term development issues for the government. These interconnected issues of development and diversification will be the focus of Chapters 4 and 5.

4 Development Planning: Contexts, Models and Institutions

Development planning in Brunei has been shaped by a range of institutional, historical and ideological factors. The particular path to independence adopted by Brunei coupled with its distinctive political structure, has bequeathed planning models and structures which reflect the strong British involvement in early planning policy in the state. At the same time, the post-independence period has been marked by a conscious effort to fashion both an individual development path for the state, and to create a range of institutions which seek to be distinctively Bruneian in scope and format. This chapter outlines the evolution and objectives of development planning in the state. Firstly, it examines the structures and institutions which shape the planning process. Secondly, it will focus on attempts to define a particular development model in the light of the economic experience of some of its Asian neighbours, and the particular religious and cultural characteristics of Brunei. After a review of the fiscal conditions underpinning development planning, a third section reviews the six National Development Plans enacted to date.

4.1 DEVELOPMENT PLANNING

It may be argued that a primary role of development planning is to provide a range of institutions and mechanisms which can guide economic performance in conjunction with market mechanisms, in ways which reflect the preferences of particular societies. In economic terms, a first aim is to ensure that scarce resources — physical, economic and human — are channelled to the most productive uses. Development planning thus reflects a deliberate attempt by government to coordinate economic decision-making over the longer term and to influence national economic growth in order to achieve a predetermined set of development objectives. The mobilisation, organisation and maximum utilisation of

all available resources is a key function of planning (Todaro, 1989;
Osama, 1987).

The planning process usually involves the selection of objectives,
setting of targets and the implementation and coordination of a development plan. It usually consists of two basic stages (Waterson, 1972). First
is the elaboration of an aggregate growth model which seeks to examine
the entire economy in terms of a limited set of macro-economic variables. These variables are those deemed most critical to the determina-
tion of growth rates of national output in areas such as investment,
money supply, savings and trade. Second is the development of multi-
sector, input-output models which ascertain the production, resource,
employment and foreign exchange implications of a given set of final
demand targets within an internally consistent framework of interindus-
try product flows. These models are more relevant to countries with a
sizeable industrial base. Thus, whilst these macro-growth models set the
broad strategy, sectoral targets and project appraisal, the more usual
form of development planning in Brunei, provide the important micro-
scale aspects of the process. The degree to which these stages in development planning are realised determines, to a large extent, the success
of the planning exercise.

In the case of Brunei, the planning process has sought to face up to
the central development issue in the state: how to make the best long-
term use of a finite resource. Like many of the oil-exporting countries
of the Middle East, the structures of development planning in Brunei
have largely followed western models. Development planning, notes
Osama (1987, 10), is concerned 'with all phases of the formulation of
policies conducive to the achievement of specific aims, and the
mobilisation, organisation and maximum utilisation of all available
resources with the purpose of realising these aims'. A primary problem in both elaborating and assessing development plans has been a
lack of detailed data. As noted in the introduction, publicly available
information is, by and large, inadequate to allow a full evaluation of
the underlying macro-economic assumptions which drive the development process. The analysis pursued here is thus focused on questions of sectoral allocations and overall economic strategy rather than
on the detailed growth models used within Treasury. In addition, an
attempt is made to situate the particular experience of Brunei within
the range of development models that have been important in the
region.

4.2 THE SEARCH FOR A DEVELOPMENT MODEL

The evolution of development planning in Brunei has reflected a number of specific development issues and models. Three in particular are highlighted here: the example of East Asian development models, the impact of size and geography on development objectives, and the effects of resource booms on the fiscal and economic conditions underpinning development strategies.

Perhaps one of the most formative and influential development models in recent decades has been that of the 'four tigers' of East Asia — the Newly Industrialising Economies (NIEs) of Singapore, Taiwan, South Korea and Hong Kong. The success of the NIEs owed much to the favourable world economic environment from the mid-1960s to the early 1970s which helped provide buoyant demand for absorbing NIE manufactured exports. The internal characteristics of the NIEs were also significant with high levels of educational attainment, a timely shift from import-substitution to export-oriented industrial strategies, and a high degree of state intervention either directly (through, for example, industrial subsidies) or indirectly (through infrastructural projects or social legislation). A general scarcity of resources has been one notable factor underlying the export-orientation policies.

Clearly, the differences between the Asian NIEs and Brunei outweigh any similarities; Brunei cannot attempt to emulate en bloc the NIE experience. However, aspects of Bruneian strategy do seek to follow the Singapore experience. Both may be regarded as micro-states. A tradition of association exists between the two countries, reflected in the exchange parity between the countries, and built on a common heritage of British influence and control. Not only has the Singapore experience of planned industrialisation been of interest to Brunei planners, but Singaporean investment planners have helped in diversifying Brunei's investment portfolios. Recent evidence from the Fifth National Development Plan (henceforth NDP 5) and NDP 6 suggests that Bruneian planners have consciously sought to develop a limited degree of industrialisation based, in the early stages at least, on import-substitution. The Brunei market, though small, is wealthy with high per capita income levels. These incomes have, since the mid-1970s stimulated a surge in imports of consumer durables, clothing, food, and beverages. The production of some of these, it is argued, could be met by domestic industry. Areas such as food processing and packaging and pharmaceuticals have been seen by Ameer Ali as offering good potential for growth. In his view (1992, 199), a closer analysis of import patterns 'invalidates the argument that industries cannot grow in Brunei because of its market constraints ... the real impediments to industrial growth should be sought in the other two constraints namely, supply and labour'. These aspects are examined further in Chapter 5.

Size and geography have framed a series of constraints on the objectives and implementation of development planning. Brunei is a tiny state of around 5,800 sq. km. It is non-contiguous, with the Temburong District accessible only by boat or air from the rest of the country. Population and services are furthermore geographically uneven. The Temburong District is thinly-peopled and poorly serviced by road; within the rest of Brunei, growth and development is polarised along a thin coastal strip. The road linking Bandar Seri Begawan through Tutong and on to Seria and Kuala Belait provides a corridor of growth with the highest development taking place at either end. The capital has grown apace in recent decades; the oil towns of Seria and Kuala Belait have provided a second focus of growth, although Kuala Belait is beginning to stagnate. Inland from the coastal corridor, settlement is scattered and population sparse with large areas of primary tropical rainforest, especially in the Temburong. Around three-quarters of the state remains under such primary forest cover; bans on commercial logging have meant that the area of cover is likely to remain high.

Small states often face a number of common development problems. Their limited range of environments can restrict both the quantity and variety of natural resource endowments, whilst small states may also have increased vulnerability to natural disasters such as cyclones, typhoons or severe flooding. Brunei has largely escaped such problems; its oil revenues reduce dependence on agricultural commodities as a source of export revenue. The impact of pollution problems in the state might pose potential threats; thus far, oil pollution has been restricted and there have been no serious oil spillage problems from offshore installations (Goh, 1992). The potential threat of pollution within Brunei Bay, shared by Brunei and the Malaysian states of Sabah and Sarawak, has thus far been averted (periodic algal blooms have, however, hit the local shellfish industry); an international management plan is currently in place for the Bay.

Perhaps more significant from the development perspective are the human resource constraints implied by small size. Small populations provide only restricted domestic markets. Even if those markets are wealthy, as in the case of Brunei, size nevertheless hampers the elaboration of import-substitution policies for developing domestic industry. The small population can also result in high unit costs for services and infrastructure because of the absence of scale economies. To some extent such costs are disguised in the case of Brunei because of its large budget surpluses. Thus the real costs of constructing a gas pipeline linking the Lumut refracting plant with the electricity generating station at Gadong (which provides electricity for the capital) were disguised by both government subsidies and by subsidies from Brunei Shell. Similarly the real costs of constructing and maintaining road networks in the state are very high and those costs are not reflected in, for example, levels of vehicle taxation. The costs of medical and educational provision are also accentuated by the small population, as well as by its scattered distribution in interior areas.

A third area in which the experiences of Brunei have been replicated in other countries concerns the impact of economic booms based on resource extraction. The preponderant place of hydrocarbons in the export and revenue profiles of Brunei mirror those of a number of other countries, most notably the smaller, Middle Eastern oil producing states. The conditions underlying economic development in such states following the oil price rises of 1973–4 and 1979–80 has spawned a number of studies examining the fiscal and development implications of the huge revenues accruing to government. Gelb (1988, 5–6) has usefully distinguished two groups of countries in his analysis of oil revenue changes. First are those he terms 'capital-deficit developing exporters' such as Algeria, Mexico or Indonesia. To such countries oil exports represent a large share of exports but relatively modest shares of gross national product. Oil output and reserves, whilst significant, 'are insufficient to bear the burden of financing development for more than another fifteen to twenty-five years unless real oil prices exhibit a rising secular trend'. The second category, into which Brunei fits, 'capital-surplus oil exporters', are countries with small populations, weakly developed domestic industry and the ability to fund a wide range of development projects from oil income alone. Countries such as pre-Gulf War Kuwait and Bahrain would also fit this category. Their problem, notes Gelb (1988, 6), is that of choosing 'an optimal asset portfolio of oil in the ground and real assets abroad'.

Both fiscal and development policy in Brunei have therefore been framed within debates about the relationship between oil output, royalty and tax revenues, overseas and domestic investment, and the growth of the non-oil sector in the country. Questions concerning rates of oil depletion, royalty, taxation and production-sharing agreements, the balance between foreign and domestic assets, and the types of strategies required to stimulate non-oil related economic growth and diversify the economy are relevant to a number of countries and have elicited a range of arguments and models.

Most attention has focused on the relationship between oil revenues and development. The link between windfall profits accruing from oil exports post-1973, and a balanced pattern (both in time and space) of economic development, can at best be described as equivocal. In examining the impact of commodity booms generally, Cuddington (1989) has highlighted the significant deficiencies that often occur in the management of windfall revenues, deficiencies which can have detrimental medium and long-term impacts. For Gelb (1988, 33), 'a positive, causal link between high-rent activities [such as an oil-price boom] and development is certainly not inevitable ... the high-rent sector may inhibit the accumulation and upgrading of reproducible factors of production, and ... in the long-term this diversion of resources and attention can stultify growth'. In their survey of a number of experiences of commodity booms, Neary and Van Wijnbergen (1986, 1) argued that 'the macroeconomic performance of many countries with large resource sectors has been less than satisfactory'.

The supposedly detrimental effects of commodity booms on the macro-economy have often been referred to as the Dutch disease, after a number of studies of the economic impact of hydrocarbon revenues in the Netherlands in the mid-1960s (Corden, 1984). In general, it is argued that a large rise in royalty and tax revenues stimulated by sharp price rises for hydrocarbons can have considerable negative impacts on growth rates for domestic agriculture and manufacturing, and on the non-tradable sector (transport, services, utilities) of the economy. This arises in part from currency appreciation, usually the favoured government policy to ensure the maximum absorption of revenue from the commodity boom into the domestic economy. As a result of this appreciation, domestic manufacturing industry finds its exports becoming less competitive and suffers competition from the lower real cost of competing imports. The agricultural sector suffers in a similar manner with a loss of both competitiveness and labour. Alongside these macro-economic impacts, increased government revenues accruing from commodity booms are frequently invested in so-called 'non-productive' sectors of the economy such as defence or social welfare. As Gelb (in Neary and Van Wijnbergen, 1986, 56) argues, 'a dominant common feature has been the speedy use of oil rents to fund domestic, and overwhelmingly public, capital formation'.

In a recent study of the Malaysian state of Sabah, which has experienced commodity booms in both oil and timber in recent years, Lim (1990) has pointed to two, interconnected manifestations of Dutch disease. First, he identified a sharp rise in demand for non-tradables (notably construction and services) to meet the demands of the booming export commodity sectors. As the supply of these non-tradables within a small underdeveloped economy is, in the short term at least, inelastic, increased imports are used to meet demand. These imports have served, in turn, to adversely affect the domestic manufacturing and agricultural sectors. A second effect, what he terms the 'resource movement', is the shift of labour from lagging local manufacturing and agricultural sectors to the export commodity sector where wages are higher and opportunities for employment greater. Lim's conclusions highlight the importance of government strategies towards currency appreciation, domestic money supply and the protection of domestic industry. Despite weaknesses in the model, he argues (1990, 152) that it represents 'a useful framework for analysing the role of government expenditure policies when there is a resource boom, especially in those countries where the revenue from the resources boom accrues mainly to government'.

A second case study, that of Kuwait prior to the Iraqi invasion in 1990, also makes comparisons apposite to the case of Brunei. Looney (1991) has pointed out that in those countries where the manufacturing base is already weak, the negative impacts of oil revenues on manufacturing will be small. In some instances currency appreciation may actually make the establishment of domestic industry more rather than less viable, by reducing the real costs of imported capital equipment. Interestingly, however, his empirical study did reveal that currency appreciation was a significant factor in reducing the competitiveness of manufacturing industry; its impact on agriculture and fisheries was, however, less than might have been expected. To what extent, then, are such examples relevant to the case of Brunei?

Initially it should be noted that it is not easy to isolate the specific effects of oil revenues on the Brunei currency. In general, the currencies of the oil-producing countries of the Middle East, with whom Brunei shares certain characteristics, tend to have overvalued currencies in order to maximise foreign exchange receipts. The value of the Brunei dollar is generally higher than its ASEAN counterparts; this may, however, reflect changes in the relative strength of the Singapore dollar with which the Brunei dollar has parity.

There may be a good case, however, for viewing some of the fiscal and economic characteristics of the state from the perspective of the Dutch disease literature. Much of the windfall profit from oil has found its way into an expanded public sector which has wages and conditions difficult to match in the private sector. Domestic manufacturing is restricted and, as the following chapter suggests, difficult to develop. High wages in the public sector are, in part, responsible for this. Brunei relies heavily on importing capital goods; an overvalued currency and smooth trading and financial flows with Singapore facilitate such imports. The small size of the domestic market is a further disincentive for manufacturing growth in the state. In addition agriculture is very poorly developed. Employment in agriculture has fallen from around one-third of the active population in 1960 to around 3 per cent in 1991 with a strong 'resource shift' of workers to employment in the oil sector or, more especially, the public sector.

Much of the ongoing debate concerning the models of economic development to be pursued by state planners have been framed within conventional western economics. With independence in Brunei, has come a greater awareness of what makes Brunei especially distinct, namely the emphasis given to Islam in daily life. The concept of the Malay Islamic Monarchy (MIB) noted in Chapter 2 has been given renewed focus in recent years. MIB 'calls for the society to be loyal to its ruler, practise Islam and make it a way of life' (*Brunei Darussalam Newsletter,* 1991) in the state. One of its implicit aims is to seek to manage the rapid societal changes that have accompanied the influx of oil revenues. Not suprisingly, Islamic precepts are likely to play an increasingly important role in the elaboration of development plans.

4.3   THE ORGANISATION OF DEVELOPMENT PLANNING

Decisions about the nature, approval and implementation of development planning in Brunei rest ultimately with the Sultan, acting in Council. Prior to self-government in 1959, a degree of control was exercised by the British government acting through the Resident. After 1959 control rested entirely with the Council; the establishment of a Cabinet system of government in 1984 did not materially change the nature of decision-making. The Sultan himself makes the final decision concerning approval for budgets, development plans and project implementation.

In the early period of development planning (the first Five Year plan was formulated in 1954) the responsibility for formulating and coordinating planning rested with a committee established from a number of ministries; the administration had no separate body charged with the formulation and execution of development policy. Development planning was controlled through coordination between a range of ministries with ultimate financial control resting with Treasury. Much development planning in the pre-independence period was carried out by external consultants or by expatriate officers of the Foreign and Commonwealth Office in London. Such a situation meant that for a number of the early National Development Plans, financial control in particular was lax. More often than not, such laxity was reflected in budget underspending as allocated projects fell behind schedule. This was especially the case with some of the larger infrastructural projects where control over labour and material supply was often inadequate.

In 1973 the Economic Planning Unit (EPU) was set up to try and rectify this situation. Established within the Ministry of Finance, the EPU was responsible for compiling, coordinating and monitoring development planning in the state. It has a statutory right to information from businesses established in Brunei and its statistical section compiles a range of information on business conditions in the state. Alongside the EPU, three other bodies within the Ministry of Finance play a role in coordinating general development policies whilst the Ministries of Development and of Industry and Primary Resources also have an input into development planning (Figure 4.1). The Economic Development Board (EDB), modelled on Singapore's Board, is primarily responsible for elaborating and administering programmes to encourage private local and foreign investment in the state. It is able to provide tax relief for certain industries granted special status, it can enter into joint venture agreements and is empowered to make loans available to Bruneian citizens to encourage business expansion. It can also purchase, hold and lease land for industrial purposes (Chi Seck Choo, 1991, 290). The EDB also monitors the insurance industry in Brunei and a recently established Tourism Promotion Committee has been seeking ways of encouraging tourism in the state.

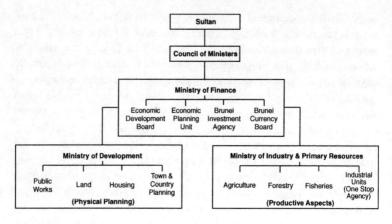

*Fig*ure 4.1   Ministries with direct involvement in development issues

The Brunei Currency Board, established in 1967, has responsibility for controlling the circulation of currency and ensuring adequate asset levels in local banks. It is also the principal licensing and monitoring agency for all the country's banks and finance companies and coordinates the actions of the Bank Supervision Unit within the Ministry of Finance. The Currency Board also plays a key role in maintaining currency interchangeability with Singapore. Under the terms of an agreement signed in June 1967 the two currencies are interchangeable at par and are accepted in either state. The agreement provides the basis upon which banks in Brunei are able to shift funds into Singapore without running the risk of currency fluctuations; this has been especially important in managing the huge funds flowing from oil revenues, most of which are channelled through Singapore. Exchange control regulations operated in Brunei prior to independence as part of a block of so-called Scheduled Territories tied to sterling. In 1984 currency conversion approval by the Board was eliminated, giving the state the necessary flexibility to conduct international transactions without any bureaucratic delays (ASEAN, 1991). The Brunei Investment Agency is responsible for investment strategies for the large accumulated surpluses of the state; its role is considered in Chapter 5.

As part of the Fifth National Development Plan two further bodies were established in 1989 to focus on development concerns. The creation of a fully-fledged Ministry of Industry and Primary Resources, with full status in Cabinet, marked a considerable upgrading of industrial and development issues. All matters relating to the creation of new industries, the diversification of the industrial base and the coordination of industrial strategy now fall within the remit of the new Ministry. As well as dealing with agriculture, forestry and fisheries, the Ministry has established a new unit — the One Stop Agency — to facilitate inward investment and the establishment of new businesses

4.4 FISCAL AND ECONOMIC GROWTH

The revenues required to maintain the high levels of public expenditure in Brunei have come entirely from hydrocarbons. The radical shifts in oil and gas prices over the last two decades have been a constant underlying factor in the structure and evolution of development plans in the state. As Chapter 3 showed, between October 1973 and February 1974 oil prices quadrupled. In late 1979 the Iran–Iraq War led to a further tripling of oil prices. Average F.O.B. prices for crude oil at Seria rose from US$2.39 in 1971 to US$11.93 in 1974 and US$38.15 in 1981. The net impact on government revenue in Brunei was phenomenal as prices rose and new offshore sources of both petroleum and gas came onstream.

The fiscal implications of the oil price changes on government revenues are shown in Table 4.1. The annual financial statistics of the state usually appear some 18 months after the end of the financial year. Government revenues are broken down into four major classes:

1. Duties, taxes and licenses which include hydrocarbon revenues
2. Receipts from various government services such as hospital or school fees
3. Receipts from the commercial arms of government such as the Lands and Survey Department
4. Receipts from government property which is composed largely of dividends and interest payments on investments together with rentals from government property.

Table 4.1 indicates the broad secular trends in revenue but requires some qualification. Of particular concern have been changes in the reporting of revenues in this period. The most important of these was the decision in 1986 to exclude revenues from foreign investments in

Table 4.1 Government revenue, 1973–90 (million dollars)

Year	1973	1974	1975	1976	1977	1978	1979	1980	1981	1982	1983	1984	1985	1986	1987	1988	1989	1990
Total	369	1 027	1 564	2 136	2 142	2 466	3238	6 266	8 454	7 871	7 752	7 344	7 532	3 331	2 750	2 486	2 525	2 796
Class 1	246	704	1 075	1 056	1 186	1 309	1 754	2 893	3 522	3 380	2 856	2 486	2 578	1 980	1 622	1 492	1 567	1 610
Class 2	0.3	0.4	0.6	0.7	0.8	1	0.6	1.3	1.4	1.7	1.7	3.6	3.9	4.6	4.3	4.5	4.5	4.4
Class 3	16	17	19	24	29	36	34	46	57	76	187	94	111	122	133	154	177	175
Class 4	105	305	468	1 054	925	1 118	1 448	3 324	4 872	4 413	4 707	4 760	4 838	1 223	989	834	776	916

Source: Treasury Department, Ministry of Finance.

overall revenue tables. The decision coincided with the removal of most of the state's investment portfolios from the British Crown Agents and their placing with the Brunei Investment Agency and a number of Japanese and American Investment Houses. The 'disappearance' of some $4 billion from the revenue account in 1986 reflected this decision. Its net effect was to show a major change in the revenue/ expenditure balance which, on closer scrutiny, was more apparent than real. Oil prices did fall in that year, but it was probably accounting practice, rather than revenue declines, which lay behind the change.

The clear boosts to government revenue in 1974 and 1979–80 are highlighted. The earlier rise can be clearly attributed to an increase in royalties and taxes from hydrocarbons due both to price rises and the coming onstream of LNG exports to Japan. For 1979–80 the picture was more complex. Between 1979 and 1981, revenues from duties rose by about 100 per cent whilst total revenue rose by 160 per cent; much of that increase came from a sizeable rise in investment revenues with overseas investments deposits more than doubling in the period. Sizeable investment in overseas equity markets were also begun in 1980. Thus between 1980 and 1985 government revenues from duties, taxes and licences remained broadly comparable whilst revenues from investments increased by almost one-third. After the accounting change in 1986, published total revenues fell dramatically from over $7 billion in 1985 to $3.3 billion in 1986 with a further fall to $2.7 billion in 1990. Hydrocarbon revenues from royalties and taxes accounted for around 60 per cent of that total. In the absence of published figures it is difficult to estimate the contribution of investment incomes. With estimated investments of around $30 billion, annual investment revenues of between $2 billion and $3 billion are likely to be flowing into Treasury, even after account is taken of the stock market falls of late 1987. With this approximate total incorporated into the revenue accounts, it can be argued that overall revenues in the 1980s have been around $7 billion per year.

The changes in accounting procedures has meant that it is more difficult to estimate the importance of revenues from hydrocarbons in the overall pattern of government income. If estimated investment incomes are included, hydrocarbon taxes and royalties accounted for about 40 per cent of the total in 1990; omitting these investments raises the proportional significance to about 60 per cent . A number of other revenue trends are worth noting. There has been a steady rise in revenue accruing to government through user-pays charging reflecting at least a

degree of commercial orientation in government departments. But the
amounts raised from such sources are tiny by comparison with other
income sources.

Expenditure patterns have been tabulated in Table 4.2. Three categor-
ies are recorded: charged expenditure (primarily official state expenditure), ordinary expenditure (that incurred by government departments)
and development expenditure (that allotted to the 5-year development
plans). Overall expenditure increased five-fold in the course of the
1970s; even accounting for inflation, this rise represented a huge real
increase in spending, reflecting the greatly increased resources of the
state. In the early 1980s, a further large rise in expenditure took place. A
dramatic increase in charged expenditure occurred, rising from $53 mil-
lion in 1982 to $2.6 billion in 1983 and $2.3 billion in 1985. Much of
this increase was linked to the large amounts of public construction
associated with Brunei's independence. The spectacularly lavish Istana
Nurul Iman, the main palace of the Sultan outside Bandar Seri
Begawan, and intended as a physical symbol of the new status of both
state and ruler, typified such construction.

Figure 4. 2 indicates the breakdown of expenditure for some of the
main votes. It shows the expanding provision for defence (especially in
the late 1970s), education and social services and public works. Defence
expenditure has focused on two areas: the costs of upkeep for the
Ghurka Batallion maintained by Brunei, largely to guard the oil and gas
installations and the continued upgrading of the Royal Brunei Armed
Forces in terms of both equipment and personnel (Huxley, 1987). The
purchase of 16 Hawk fighter aircraft in 1991 signals an intention to
develop a fixed wing airforce in the state. Close institutional and physical links are maintained with the British army (whose officers and advi-
sors work in the state) and with the armed forces of Singapore, who
benefit from jungle training facilities in Temburong. The recent growth
in public works expenditure reflects in part the continued expansion of
public housing schemes in the capital. In an effort to move people out of
the traditional Kampong Ayer (the water village at the heart of the
capital), a range of government-sponsored housing estates have been
developed on the outskirts of the city (Cleary and Kam, 1992). These
can be purchased through subsidised mortgage schemes although, in
general, only the better-off public servants are able to take advantage of
the schemes because of the level of income requirements. Finally, the
education budget has grown in the last decade with an upgrading of

Table 4.2   Government expenditure, 1973–90 (million dollars)

Year	1973	1974	1975	1976	1977	1978	1979	1980	1981	1982	1983	1984	1985	1986	1987	1988	1989	1990
Total	226	283	481	590	640	743	1050	1140	1377	1742	4457	4136	4317	2720	2434	2721	2846	2790
Charged	8.4	9.9	22.0	26.2	33.4	35.7	51.5	44.7	51.5	53.9	2635.4	1483.4	2386.7	467.5	420.6	399.3	427.8	458.0
Ordinary	172.4	226.7	370.8	448.2	520.3	623.6	839.3	920.3	1126	1311.0	1346.4	2312.4	1599.4	1873.7	1674.3	1945.6	1876.9	1870.5
Dev.	45.5	46.9	88.0	115.7	86.7	83.7	159.2	175.7	200.1	377.0	475.1	341.5	331.7	379.0	339.5	376.4	496.4	461.9

Source: Treasury Department: Ministry of Finance.

Note: Totals have been rounded.

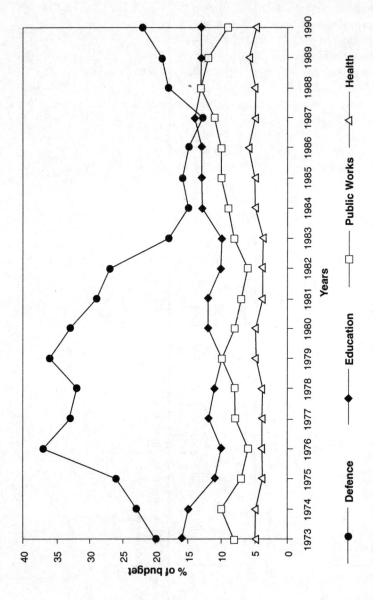

Figure 4.2   Government expenditure patterns, 1973–90.

educational provision. This has mainly been in the tertiary sector. Considerable numbers of young Bruneians train abroad, primarily in the United Kingdom; the establishment of a new University in 1986 and the upgrading of the main Institute of Technology reflect a desire to create national educational institutions. Given the small size of the population, such institutions are expensive to establish and maintain.

As Table 4.3 indicates, the national budget has been well in surplus for most of the post-1973 period; the small deficits recorded since 1988 reflect changes in accounting procedure rather than fundamental revenue or expenditure shifts. These accumulated surpluses mean that Brunei, not suprisingly, has no foreign debt.

The major period of growth in Brunei's Gross Domestic Product was between 1974 and 1979 when average annual growth rates of over 11 per cent were recorded. Changes in GDP closely reflect shifts in hydrocarbon prices; since the early 1980s GDP in real terms has stagnated or

Table 4.3   Government surplus/deficit after currency adjustment,1973–90 (million dollars)

Year	Surplus (+)/deficit (−)
1973	+ 0.07
1974	+ 0.714
1975	+ 0.955
1976	+1.170
1977	+1.600
1978	+1.764
1979	+2.140
1980	+5.051*
1981	+5.406
1982	+6.639
1983	+4.344
1984	+2.447*
1985	+3.346*
1986	+0.579*
1987	+0.355*
1988	−0.388
1989	−0.351
1990	−0.022

* Does not take account of currency adjustment.

Source: Treasury Department: Ministry of Finance.

declined. As Table 4.4 emphasises, the oil and gas sector has been the key determinant of GDP changes, a fact which has rendered government efforts to diversify all the more important. The contribution of the non-oil sector has risen steadily from around 17 per cent in 1977 to 28 per cent in 1983 and 57 per cent in 1990. This change reflects, to a large degree, changes in GDP induced by government expenditure: at constant prices, this rose from 9.2 per cent in 1983 to 22 per cent in 1990. However, since much of that government expenditure is sourced from either hydrocarbon or investment revenues, the extent of non-oil GDP is more apparent than real. Much of that expenditure has gone into the construction sector with major housing and infrastructural projects and in the provision of a range of social and personal services. The contribution of the latter to GDP rose from 5 per cent in 1977 to 20 per cent in 1988.

The evolution of per capita GDP has reflected two factors, fluctuations in hydrocarbon production and prices, and population change. Per capita GDP was about $4,200 in 1971. It rose rapidly to $25,521 in 1978 and a peak of $56,979 in 1980. Since then population increase and the levelling of hydrocarbon prices has led to a decline. In 1990 it stood at about $17,000, still one of the highest in the region. The decline in per capita figures has not necessarily been reflected in changed living standards; revenues have remained buoyant, as was noted earlier, and the continued high rate of investment in community and personal social

Table 4.4   Contribution to gross domestic product of selected economic activities 1977–88 (% at constant 1974 prices)

	1977	*1980*	*1983*	*1986*	*1988*
Agric., forestry fisheries	0.96%	0.99%	1.14%	1.39%	1.30%
Mining and manufacturing	83.4%	78.9%	72.3%	66.4%	60.2%
Construction	1.94%	2.31%	3.45%	1.97%	1.90%
Wholesale, retail trade	5.84%	8.09%	8.39%	6.96%	7.89%
Community, social and personal services	5.07%	6.46%	9.36%	16.73%	20.49%

Source: Brunei Statistical Yearbooks.

services has helped in maintaining living standards. As Moehammad Nazir (1990, 54) notes, falling oil prices did not result 'in direct repercussions on domestic private consumption expenditure'. It is difficult to obtain precise data on income inequality in the country. Arief (1986, ch. 9) identified high income inequality with a Gini-coefficient of 0.56 in the early-1980s. A study by the EPU in 1986 also found a high degree of inequality with the top 10 per cent of income earners accounting for over 40 per cent of all income. A Gini-coefficient of 0.46 was calculated from this data (Moehammad Nazir, 1990; Haji Ismail bin Haji Duraman, 1990).

As was noted earlier, Brunei has experienced a high rate of demographic growth in the last two decades, with rates in excess of 2 per cent per year. The Brunei Darussalam Master Plan of 1986 (prepared by consultants Huszar Brammah and Associates) suggested that by the year 2005 the total population of the state would be around 364,000 compared with the 1991 population of 260,000. Under three different scenarios, however, the size of the immigrant population, a critical labour source in Brunei, varied between 40,000 and 94,200, depending on the demand parameters used in the model. Brunei relies very heavily on immigrant labour for both skilled technical and managerial positions and for the lower-paid retailing and construction sectors. Even if the lowest scenario for total labour demand is assumed a sizeable immigrant labour force would still be required to meet demand for workers from sectors which are likely to remain unattractive to the citizen population. The estimated doubling of the permanent labour force between 1985 and 2005 underlines the central importance of job creation strategies for planners in the state.

4.5   THE DEVELOPMENT PLANS: A SYNOPSIS

Contemporary economic and social development policies in Brunei are formulated within the framework of development planning which, at best, should represent an organised, conscious and continued attempt to select the best available alternatives for achieving specific goals (Waterson, 1972). Through planning policies, development can be coordinated and, in principle, the appropriate mix of public and private enterprise and the requisite rates of economic growth can be planned. Development planning in Brunei is macro, multi-sectoral and project-based and has historically taken the form of five-year development plans. A brief synopsis of these plans is provided in this section.

4.5.1   First Five Year Development Plan (1953–8)

The first five year national development plan (NDP 1) was drawn up under the close scrutiny of the Colonial Office and most of the staff responsible for compiling and monitoring the plan were British expatriate staff. The fiscal context of the plan was a steady increase in oil revenues from the expanding Seria field. The plan was rudimentary in nature and consisted largely of a series of infrastructural projects. The total sum allocated to the plan was $100 million over the five year period; by the end of 1958 around 75 per cent of that had been spent. However, the somewhat *ad hoc* nature of the plan is underscored by the fact that the final programme and budget for NDP 1 was not published until 1958! The main focus of the plan was two-fold: infrastructural development and the expansion of social services.

About 80 per cent of the budget was allocated for infrastructure with the bulk of expenditure on road construction and public utilities. A plan for the resettlement of Kampong Ayer was put forward and funding allocated for the provision of land for those inhabitants wishing to resettle. Efforts were also made to encourage diversification. Irrigation projects and the development of a nursery for rubber seedlings were planned for the agricultural sector. The port wharves at Kuala Belait and Brunei were to be improved and a major project, finally completed on Christmas Day 1958 was the opening of the Brunei Town-Seria link road which finally facilitated smooth communications between the capital and the oil installations. The construction of road bridges over the Tutong and Telamba Rivers eliminated long waits for ferries at Kuala Tutong and Danau. Social provisions were also included in the plan. A pensions and disability allowance scheme was instituted and plans for a new hospital at Kuala Belait and some thirty new schools were put forward.

The plan was fairly vague and no clear proposals for monitoring its progress were laid down, making it difficult to evaluate its success. In some areas — pensions, the new hospital, communications, real progress was made. In agriculture considerable investments were made in infrastructural facilities (irrigation, drainage, research facilities) and providing subsidies for crop cultivation. In others, most notably in expanding non-oil related industry, little was actually done. If the accounting systems of the period made a distinction between development and current expenditure, in practice the distinction hardly operated. The example of social services provision illustrates this. Under NDP 1 about 20 per cent of the development budget was allocated to health and educational provision but, examining the accounts of the period, it is largely impossible to disentangle current and development expenditure on these areas. Accounting procedures were often rudimentary as was the data base on which financial assessments were made. Economic planning, notes Ameer Ali (1992), was purely experimental in nature during these early years.

4.5.2 Second Five Year Development Plan (NDP 2, 1962–6)

The launching of NDP 2 some 4 years after NDP 1 had ended marked the start of effective development planning in the state. A Planning Committee from the different Ministries was charged with framing a five-year development plan with a range of economic, social and cultural elements. Eight advisory groups were involved in the drafting of the plan. The plan lacked detailed examination of particular projects. As the preamble stated, 'there is still further action to be taken. Study in detail of each programme and project has to be undertaken with the view to determine its cost and facilitate budget preparation'. The plan included a statement of objectives, a consideration of the macroeconomic environment for development, and a preliminary list of projects deemed to form part of the programme.

Diversification and reduction of disparities in regional growth were key economic objectives specified in the plan. High priority was given to securing a sustained increase in per capita GDP. Greater equity in income distribution, the creation of a comprehensive system of education and a national health service were also listed as key aims. The plan recognised the limitations of development planning noting that it served 'to indicate the direction only, not the speed of development' and that the fulfillment of the stated objectives would not be achieved within the five year period.

The key focus of the programme was on the provision of the necessary economic and social infrastructure in the state together with specific economic targets. Two were especially important: to reverse the declining GNP growth rate, and to increase per capita GNP growth to at least 4 per cent per year. The reasons for the decline in GNP were specified in the plan. A fall in the rate of investment by government was identified as being especially important, and the tapering off of NDP 1 and delays in establishing NDP 2 were seen as contributing factors. As a result, increased investment by the state was seen as critical to the success of the NDP 2 programme. An estimated investment of 12 to 14 per cent of GNP was postulated as being necessary to secure expansion in the economy. Most of this investment, it was suggested, would have to be met by the public sector. NDP 2 was much more explicit than NDP 1 in terms of budgets and projects with a large number of itemised projects. However a development budget was prepared only for the first year of the plan on the grounds that budgeting for future years was impossible without adequate data to facilitate the exercise.

NDP 2 identified a number of key areas for attention. Increasing the output of agriculture was seen as especially important and a range of pilot projects for both new crops (coffee, groundnuts, maize) and existing crops were proposed. Improvements in fishery and forest production were also advocated. As with NDP 1 expenditure on transport, communications and infrastructure was high: about 54 per cent of total expenditure under the plan went to these projects. Included here were projects to improve the Muara port and to facilitate better telecommunications in the state. A number of potential areas for manufacturing growth were noted with feasibility studies proposed for developing the use of glass sand deposits, timber processing and fertilisers. Education and housing were the largest recipients of funding after infrastructure; the amounts allocated to agriculture or industrial development were small

NDP 2 lasted far longer than originally anticipated and some of the specified activities continued through until late-1972. The total budget was $492 million but, as with the first plan, budget control was weak and many projects, especially in the construction sector, took far longer than anticipated. During the course of NDP 2 there were major expansions of expenditure in the field of education (the development budget allocations for education, for example, increased eight-fold in the period 1966–8) and public works. Much of the expenditure in the latter was devoted to housing construction for an increasing number of government staff together with major construction and remedial work on the Berakas Army Camp close to the capital. Overall, in the defined period of the plan, GDP rose by around 6.6 per cent a year, just above the rate projected in the plan: a higher than anticipated rate of population growth meant that the targeted 4 per cent growth in per capita GDP was not achieved. The plan can therefore claim some success in meeting its objectives. Communications were improved as was the provision of electricity and water. However, as NDP 3 noted, 'the Plan did not contribute significantly to the structural change or diversification of the economy with the oil industry still dominating the economic structure of the country'.

4.5.3 Third National Development Plan (1975–9)

A gap of some six years between the projected end of NDP 2 and the start of planning for NDP 3 reflected the loose framework set up for NDP 2 and the lack of strong budgetary control. NDP 3 was formulated in a period of marked economic change. Government revenues increased more than five-fold between 1973 and 1975, creating a new fiscal and economic context for development planning. The creation of the Economic Planning Unit in 1973 specifically to coordinate and monitor the devel◌pment plans created new administrative structures and presaged, in principle, much more coordinated planning efforts

The aim of diversification dominated NDP 3. Within the employment objective of creating around 10,000 new jobs over the period of the plan, it stated clearly that 'it is neither feasible nor desirable for this addition to be wholly absorbed by either the services or the mining (oil and gas) sector' (43). Structural imbalances in the economy were clearly identified as a critical problem, and developments in agriculture, forestry, fishing and manufacturing were seen as essential to the long-term health of the economy. The manufacturing sector was identified as the 'leading sector in the developing countries at this stage of development' (44) but the plan argued for the need to give support to both agriculture and manufacturing at the same time. Diversification was needed, it was argued, 'to reduce the structural imbalance' and resources had to be focused 'to accelerate the development of sectors consistent with the balanced development of the whole economy' (43). The plan further sought to achieve a 6 per cent annual growth in GDP and to maintain high levels of employment in the economy. Whilst recognising the critical importance of private enterprise, the plan underscored the continued need for major government intervention in the economy: 'the Government' it noted (47) 'will consider playing a more active and meaningful economic role than hitherto in order to give effect to the general development strategy and the optimum achievement possible of the aim and objectives of the present Plan'.

The sectoral allocations made under the plan did not necessarily reflect these stated priorities (Table 4.5). First, as Arief (1986, 19) notes, the absorption rate of expenditure was low and actual development expenditure was only 67.5 per cent of the budgeted figure, suggesting a number of infrastructural and administrative bottlenecks. A lack of proper planning and coordination between ministries, overunning in the selection and surveying of new construction sites and a lack of skilled personnel have been cited as contributory factors. Under NDP 3 the Brunei Economic Development Board was established. Modelled on the Singapore Board it was designed to attract inward and domestic investment in industrial ventures through the provision of tax privileges and other incentives.

Overall, most of the NDP 3 budget went into a familiar range of infrastructural developments including roads (11.6 per cent), telecommunications (10 per cent) and improvements in water supply (7 per cent). Other areas included upgradings in education and health. In terms of diversification policies, rhetoric was perhaps greater than investment. Agriculture, forestry and fisheries received only small sums, and continued to decline whilst the budget for industrial diversification projects was tiny. Whilst NDP 3 faced the familiar problems of monitoring and control, in some respects its stated objectives were achieved. The targeted annual growth of 6 per cent in GDP was achieved, though that growth reflected more the changes in oil prices than any dramatic

Table 4.5   Expenditure for the 3rd, 4th, 5th National Development Plans

Total budget	3rd Plan $533 554	4th Plan $1 749 814	5th Plan $2 610 000
Industry	6.6%	2.2%	10.0%
Transport and communications	33.6%	23.3%	20.0%
Social services	36.6%	28.2%	29.0%
Public utilities	20.3%	14.3%	20.0%
Public buildings	2.9%	16.4%	10.0%
Security	n.a.	15.5%	10.0%
Other	n.a.	0.1%	1.0%

Note: Figures for 3rd and 4th Plan are actual expenditure. Figures for 5th Plan are allocated expenditure.

Source: National Development Plans, Brunei Darussalam.

increase in the productive capacity of the country. Non-oil GDP remained largely unchanged at around 20 per cent whilst the GDP contribution of agriculture fell from 1.34 per cent in 1975 to 0.86 per cent in 1979. The share of the non-oil manufacturing sector also declined from 1.19 per cent in 1975 to 0.55 per cent in 1979 (Arief, 1986, 18–19), hardly satisfactory outcomes given the central diversification aim of the programme. A growth of about 4 per cent in available jobs was a satisfactory outcome, although this growth concentrated markedly in the public sector, as increased government revenues fed through into an expanding public sector, a not uncommon phenomenon in many of those oil-producing economies after the oil price rises of 1973–4. Attempts to establish a number of major industrial projects such as a pulp-mill, an ammonia-urea plant and a glass manufacturing industry were unsuccessful. As NDP 4 rather ironically noted, the high price of fuel was a contributory factor to this lack of success.

4.5.4 Fourth National Development Plan (1980–4)

The formulation of NDP 4 sought to take account of both the strengths and weaknesses of earlier plans and of a number of changes in the state itself. First, Brunei's independence in 1984 made it especially important 'to ensure and maintain peace, security and prosperity' (NDP 4, 56). Secondly, it noted the changed geo-political situation in neighbouring countries (most notably in Indo-China) which had potential consequences for rice supplies, and thirdly, perceived difficulties in obtaining cheap labour from neighbouring countries.

NDP 4 had a range of both fiscal and development objectives. The two major fiscal objectives were to secure an average annual growth rate of at least 6 per cent in GDP, and an increase in per capita income levels of at least 4 per cent per year. Alongside these objectives, NDP 4 outlined a number of other key aims. These included: the maintenance of a high level of employment; diversification through the development of agriculture and non-oil based manufacturing industry; keeping inflation within manageable levels; reducing income disparities and establishing a system of orderly rural and urban planning. In addition were a number of objectives in the social and cultural arena, notably the expansion of education at all levels and the construction of a number of rural clinics

As Table 4.5 indicates, the budget for NDP 4 almost tripled by comparison with NDP 3, a reflection, first and foremost of the greatly altered fiscal position of the state by the late 1970s. As with NDP 3, however, analysis of the sectoral allocations within the programme highlights some puzzling elements. The expenditure on programmes in industry and commerce, a key part of the diversification strategy, actually fell from around 0.9 per cent under NDP 3 to 0.3 per cent under NDP 4. Similarly, expenditure on agriculture, forestry and fisheries also declined in percentage terms from 5.7 per cent under NDP 3 to 1.9 per cent under NDP 4. The allocations to education, health and social services remained broadly similar in relative terms. Large allocations were made to public construction and security; over 31 per cent of the budget was earmarked for these items, a reflection of expenditure associated with forthcoming independence. If these large allocations are extracted from the budget, the three-fold increase by comparison with NDP 3 looks rather less impressive.

How successful, then, was NDP 4 in meeting its objectives? In terms of GDP changes, it failed, since GDP actually declined in the period by over 4 per cent per year as both oil prices and production fell. It could be argued that this change was largely beyond the control of planners. Investment rates, perhaps a better indication of the underlying impact of the plan, actually rose substantially in the period; private sector investment, for example, was actually five times higher than anticipated in the plan (Arief, 1986, 22). Employment grew by about 4.5 per cent per year; well ahead of the planned estimates of around 3.5 per cent.

4.5.5   Fifth National Development Plan (1986–90)

The stated objectives of NDP 5, the first full plan since independence, were somewhat broader than earlier ones. Estimates of GDP change were less rigidly incorporated into the plan and economic diversification policies assummed a key role. Strategies of both export-oriented industrialisation and import-substitution industrialisation were espoused in the programmes. Associated with a range of measures to diversify the economy, discussed more fully in the following chapter, came an explicit focus on the need to upgrade human resources, to nurture a new generation of Bruneian enterpreneurs and to maintain full employment.

Fundamental to NDP 5 was an increase in the size of the budget allocation for industry. Overall the development budget was increased by about 50 per cent; industrial development programmes were allocated about 10 per cent of the budget with half of this figure being set aside specifically for industrial promotion. The upgrading of public utilities to cope with the expansion of the capital and the resultant pressures on water, sewage and electricity, was also regarded as critical. NDP 5 recognised the need for a more aggressive role in attracting industry noting that it would be 'outward-looking and, where necessary, would participate actively in high-risk areas' (NDP 5, 24). Private investment, especially non-oil based investment, was estimated to increase by around 10 per cent per year, and the plan recognised the need to create a range of institutions to facilitate such investment. The establishment of a Development Bank, a National Training Scheme and a National Pension Scheme for the private sector were presaged in the plan. A range of programmes to improve human resources (the expansion of the Institute of Technology and the new University) were also to be set in train.

Detailed assessment of NDP 5 forms an important part of the NDP 6 document which at the time of writing has yet to be released to the public. In the absence of the requisite statistical information it is difficult to make an accurate assessment of the programme. A number of general observations can, however, be made. Overall, as with earlier plans, actual expenditure by government as part of NDP 5 fell short of its target. Actual expenditure, at about $2053m was around 78 per cent of targeted expenditure. However, neither the actual sectoral expenditure figures nor the estimates of private investment are yet published. The clear emphasis on diversification is to some extent supported by the available information. The contribution of the non-oil sector to GDP fell in the period 1986–1990 from 66.4 per cent to 53.0 per cent. However the extent to which manufacturing GDP rose cannot yet be estimated since the data for mining and manufacturing are amalgamated. Much of that fall may have been taken up by a marked rise in community, social and personal services, much of it stimulated by government expenditure. A rise in private sector employment from 29,973 in 1986 to 53,613 does, however, suggest some success in reducing the dependence on government employment. Some modest increases in exports of non-oil items have been recorded. Two textile factories created under the plan exported some $16m of goods to Europe and the USA in 1992, whilst plants manufacturing dairy products, canned drinks and bottled mineral water are operational. Overall GDP per capita rose during the period of the plan from $22,963 in 1986 to $29,404 in 1990.

In other areas assessment is a little easier. The objectives for human resource development included the establishment of a University and the

Institute of Technology, both of which were operative in the period of
the plan. Plans to introduce a National Pension Scheme for the private
sector labour force did not materialise in the plan period. A proposal to
establish a development bank did not materialise until late-1991, after
the end of the plan period. Some of the efforts to diversify the economy
through a range of stimuli are considered more fully in Chapter 5.

4.5.6   Sixth National Development Plan (1991–95)

At some $5.5 billion,the budget allocation for NDP 6 represented a
sizeable increase on the earlier programmes. The chief aim of the plan
was, as with NDP 5, to establish a sustainable and diverse economic
base. NDP 6 seeks to set up some 2,000 projects with job-creation as the
central objective. It is planned that these projects in the manufacturing,
financial and service sector will lead to 40,000 job opportunities over
the plan period. Allocations made under the plan, however, differ relatively little from NDP 5 making it somewhat difficult to assess the feasibility of such aims. In relative terms, the allocation for Trade and
Industry, at about 10 per cent of the total budget, remains unchanged.
Other aspects of the budget — the allocations for example, for social
services or public utilities, also differ little on relative terms from NDP
5 although the absolute budget has grown considerably.

Table 4.6 indicates the sectoral allocation of development funds
under NDP 6. As with NDP 5 much of the rhetoric in the plan proposals
is focused on the need for economic diversification. The expansion of
the non-oil sector and a reduction in dependence on government expenditure underpin the development proposals. As part of the diversification
strategy continued investment in agriculture to increase national food
security is highlighted, together with the need to develop high value-
added and capital intensive industries. An expansion of the financial
provisions for new entrepreneurs is anticipated with a continued key
role for the Economic Development Board.

The focus of the sectoral development programmes of NDP 6 is on
the non-oil private sector. The continued expansion of industrial estates
is highlighted and sustained investment in agro-industry and high value
farm products is seen as a way of improving employment prospects in
those sectors. The construction industry, in recession for much of the
late-1980s is expected to grow, particularly with the expansion of the
the National Housing Scheme. As Table 4.7 notes, over the plan period

Table 4.6   Expenditure for 6th National Development Plan

Total budget	5,509,000	
Industry		10.0%
Industrial Fund	1.8%	
Agriculture/Forestry	1.5%	
Commerce	1.0%	
Industrial Estates	3.1%	
Transport and communications		20.0%
Roads	8.9%	
Telecommunications	7.1%	
Aviations/Ports	3.2%	
Social services		29.3%
Housing	14.2%	
Education	7.0%	
Public Facilities	4.5%	
Religious Affairs	1.0%	
Public utilities		20.0%
Electricity	10.7%	
Water	5.8%	
Drainage	1.9%	
Public buildings		10.0%
Security		7.0%
Army	6.3%	
Police	0.7%	
Other		3.7%

Source: 6th National Development Plan.

some 11,000 housing units are anticipated in eight locations. Other areas of infrastructural expenditure include a major enhancement of telecommunications services and the upgrading of electricity generation and water supply.

A number of organisational changes have been introduced alongside NDP 6. A Trade and Industry Development Council was established in January 1992 charged with securing greater investment in the industrial sector. During 1992, trade and economic delegations from Japan and

Table 4.7   National housing schemes under 6th National Development Plan

District	Scheme	Target population
	Lambak Kanan	15,000
Brunei-Muara	Kampong Rimba	15,000
	Kampong Mentiri	5,000
	Kampong Pandan	10,000
Belait	Lorong Tengah	10,000
	Sungai Liang	7,000
Tutong	Bukit Beruang	8,000
Temburong	Kampong Rataie	3,000

Source: 6th National Development Plan (1991–5).

Taiwan visited the state to investigate investment opportunities and Brunei itself sent a trade delegation to Hanoi to discuss bilateral economic cooperation (Mani, 1993, 105). The expanding offshore petroleum sector in Vietnam provided opportunities for Bruneian investment through joint venture organisations. In addition, Brunei has welcomed the opportunities created through the establishment of an Asean Free Trade Area in January 1993.

4.6   PERSPECTIVES ON THE DEVELOPMENT PLANS

Whilst there has been undoubted progress in the formulation and implementation of development plans in the state over the last two decades, a number of general weaknesses are still apparent. First, it is unfortunate that, as yet, no single, overall body has been charged with all aspects of development planning. Whilst the Economic Planning Unit retains a degree of overall control, 'development' issues remain fragmented between the different ministries of government. The establishment of a Ministry of Industry and Primary Resources in 1989 has not solved this problem. Secondly, there have not been any mid-term planning reviews. In the case of Malaysia, such reviews have provided an opportunity to assess the delivery of the development programmes and examine the extent to which budgetary provisions have been met. Such reviews would provide Bruneian planners with a useful mechanism for reexamining the provisions of the five-year plans.

A third difficulty is the absence of any longer-term perspective plan. Again, the comparison with Malaysia is instructive. There, a longer-term perspective plan provides a framework within which to situate the shorter-term planning objectives of the five-year plans. It can serve to outline some of the macro-economic objectives of planners as well as providing an opportunity to develop some of the wider ideological and societal objectives that are enshrined in the more detailed planning programmes. No doubt, such a longer-term perspective plan might allow for a fuller elaboration of some of the Islamic precepts that government seeks to place at the heart of the development process.

A key element in analysing the implementation of development plans has been the important distinction between development administration, and public administration which fulfills an essentially bureaucratic role. Until 1973, that distinction hardly operated within Brunei which had no separate body to deal with development issues; ultimately control rested with Treasury whose rationale was fiscal rather than developmental. That budget underspend rather than overspend was characteristic of earlier plans may well reflect the influence of Treasury. The creation of the Economic Planning Unit in 1973 was designed to remedy this; the creation of a seperate Ministry of Development with a seat in Cabinet in 1989 should mark a further increase in control of some of the physical aspects of development policy. Nevertheless, development planning has continued to suffer from a lack of consistency between plans, and more particularly, from a failure to monitor on-going development projects. It may well be that such failures will be less likely given the emergence of a tighter development administration with an increasingly well-trained personnel. Whilst bureaucratic obstacles can still be formidable, an increasingly development-focused set of priorities is likely to ease such obstacles.

In general, three central themes in development planning may usefully be identified: objectives, requirements and constraints (Figure 4.3). It may be argued that recent economic and political trends in the state have led to a sharpening of the objectives of development planning. Government, taking its lead from the *titahs* of the Sultan is arguing for the establishment of a sustainable economy within the firm ideological framework of the Malay Islamic Monarchy. Sustainability requires economic diversification; that diversification is seen as central to a strategy of encouraging business and job creation in order to establish a secure economic base on which to build a distinctively Bruneian culture and

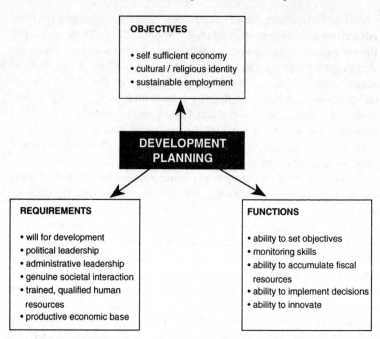

Figure 4.3   Attributes of development planning

polity. The establishment in late-1991 of the first Islamic Bank in the country may be seen as reflecting a desire to create planning systems and institutions which do not simply ape western conceptions of progress and growth.

In terms of both requirements and constraints, development planning and administration have undoubtedly progressed in Brunei. There exists a strong will for allocative forms of development, articulated by Cabinet and by an increasingly well-trained administrative cadre. In the absence of any form of elective government, however, it is difficult to judge the extent to which development planning receives popular support. In the sense that many of the outcomes of development planning, especially in the fields of health, education and public housing, are local and receive full coverage in the government-controlled media, popular support is certainly encouraged. Constraints on development planning continue to impede the full implementation of plans. Lines of responsibility are often rigid and are reinforced by an autocratic style of government and administration in which risk-taking and initiative are discouraged. The ultimate approval of development plans rests with the Sultan in Council; delays in the publication of NDP 6 illustrate the difficulties that can result.

There can be little doubt that development planning in the state has made remarkable progress in the last two decades. General policies and specific programmes are increasingly framed within the context of wider, international developmental experiences. Planning has become increasingly sophisticated and monitoring of plans, a major problem in the 1960s and 1970s has improved. The experiences of other small oil-exporting countries, critiques of western development models and the potential for a more Islamic conception of development have all influenced the shape and implementation of the national development plans. By the late 1980s, economic diversification was the leitmotiv of development planners; the following chapter examines in more detail those specific diversification programmes.

5 Diversifying the Economy

As the preceding chapter has emphasised, economic development in Brunei has depended to an inordinate degree on the revenue benefits of the hydrocarbon industry. In an attempt to reduce the heavy reliance on oil and gas revenues and returns from overseas investments, development policies in the fourth, fifth and sixth national development plans have focused on the need for economic diversification. Planners now accept that the long term growth of the economy depends on a more diversified economic base. With most of the state's food needs, machinery and equipment, intermediate materials and even labour being imported, the problems of such external dependency have become increasingly acute.

The need for access to alternative sources of income and employment has also been underlined by the medium and long-term fragility of the oil economy noted in Chapter 3. Planners and political analysts alike are aware that a prolonged slump in prices and production would threaten national revenues, increase unemployment and create political instability. The need for access to alternative sources of revenues and jobs has thus underpinned attempts to wean the economy away from its dependency on oil and gas. Diversification policies have thus been a central leitmotiv of the development debate in recent years (Cleary and Shuang Yann Wong, 1993).

This chapter is divided into three sections. The first section examines the background to the diversification debate and, more particularly, outlines some of the rationales behind those policies. A second section evaluates the achievements of the diversification strategies that have been undertaken thus far and the third section considers the prospects for sustainable economic diversification in Brunei.

5.1 THE DIVERSIFICATION DILEMMA

As Chapter 4 suggested, economic diversification has been a constant element in the development strategies pursued by the state in preparing for a non-oil future. It might be argued, however, that, at least until recent years, the development plans paid little more than lip-service to such aims, rather than elaborating clear strategies to achieve diversification. Under NDP 1 (1954–58) a diversified economic base was seen as vital; in the almost forty years since then, the achievements have been muted to say the least.

There can be little doubt that the expansion of the oil and gas industry has greatly improved the standard of living in Brunei with its revenues contributing to increased GDP, no foreign debt, a state-funded system of health and education and increases in material prosperity. Such real achievements however, cannot disguise the fact that the hydrocarbon industry alone will not be able to meet the rising demands and expectation amongst all sections of society. A changed external and internal economic environment has necessitated the diversification moves.

5.1.1 Population growth, employment and sectoral growth

The population of Brunei has been growing at an average rate of 3 per cent per annum, one of the highest growth rates in the region. The increase in population from about 88,000 in 1961 to about 260,000 in 1990 has triggered a sizeable demand for foodstuffs, services, clothing and construction which at present, are met largely by imports. Such import rises pose no difficulties for the balance of payments since hydrocarbon revenues are sufficiently high to meet import costs. In the longer term, however, problems will arise when hydrocarbon reserves are depleted or if a prolonged period of falling or low prices eventuates. The need for diversification is thus deemed necessary simply to meet the increased population of the state.

In Brunei, most employment growth over the last two decades has been in the public sector; in 1986, about 51 per cent of the labour force was employed there. Most of those employed in the public sector are citizens. The oil and gas sectors by contrast, absorbed only 6 per cent of the labour force in 1981 (Table 5.1). Oil sector employment rates are declining; in 1990 under 5 per cent of the active labour force was employed in that sector. However, the impact of the Bruneianisation programme has increased citizen employment at the expense of permanent residents and expatriates. Unemployment rates have been a cause for some alarm in political circles. The rate of unemployment almost doubled from 3.6 per cent in 1981 to 6.1 per cent in 1986 and was estimated to be over 7 per cent in 1990. The unemployment problem is structurally based and is due largely to the perception that employment

Table 5.1   Working population by sector, 1971–86

Sector	1971 No.	1971 %	1981 No.	1981 %	1986 No.	1986 %
Public	15,578	38.9	31,726	46.6	41 250	50.9
Private of which:	24,434	61.1	36,402	53.4	39 854	49.1
Oil	2,827	7.1	3,832	5.6	3 939	4.9
Total	40,012		68,128		81 104	
Unemployment rate		2.6		3.6		6.1

Source: Population Census, 1971, 1981; Population Survey, 1986.

in the private sector implies poorer wages and fringe benefits than the public sector. Notwithstanding that fact, private sector employment did double in absolute terms during the 1980s. A reduction of posts in the public and oil sectors coupled with rising unemployment has made it imperative to expedite the process of diversification.

Brunei faces potentially serious problems from the structural imbalances in its economy with agriculture and manufacturing in particular being very poorly developed. The contribution of agriculture, forestry and fishing to gross domestic product dropped from about 4 per cent in 1970 to 2 per cent in 1990. The annual growth rate of the agricultural sector during the period 1975–84 was only 0.81 per cent, indicating the limited success in fostering growth in this non-oil sector (Hamzah, 1980; Neville, 1985). Before oil was discovered in the 1930s, Brunei was close to self-sufficiency in the supply of basic foods such as rice and fish. After the oil discovery and with the increase in local population, local food production soon became inadequate to meet demand. In recent years, the expansion of population has run almost in parallel with the rise in food imports in Brunei (Table 5.2). The value of imported foodstuffs rose from B$90 million in 1975 to about B$324 million in 1988. The import value of the basic food crop, rice, almost quadrupled from about B$3 million in 1963 to B$17.6 million in 1986; the level of self-sufficiency in rice halved between 1963 (36 per cent) and 1984

Table 5.2   Population growth and food imports, 1970–90

Year	Population ('000)	Food imports ($m)
1970	130	43.3
1975	156	89.5
1980	185	183.7
1982	200	239.9
1984	216	284.4
1986	226	299.5
1988	241	324.4
1990	256	na

Source: Brunei Statistical Yearbook.

(17 per cent). For fish, a staple of the Bruneian diet, self sufficiency fell from about 60 per cent in 1975 to 30 per cent in 1990.

A number of attempts have been made to develop and diversify agriculture through promoting the cultivation of cash crops such as rubber, pepper, oil palm and cocoa. Rubber was once grown extensively, but production declined from the early 1960s as demand fell and labour shifted to the oil sector. In 1984, only 4,470 ha of rubber was left including a large number of redundant rubber smallholdings (Ministry of Development, 1986) compared to the peak of 14,000 ha in 1958. Timber has ceased to be a non-oil export item, owing to a forestry policy that seeks to conserve rainforest areas in the country. Brunei has in any case poor comparative advantages in competing with its neighbouring ASEAN counterparts in the cultivation of these cash crops. Farmers have yet to find crops that could yield wage returns comparable to those offered in the government and oil sectors. As a result cultivated land is often abandoned as in the case of rubber smallholdings which have turned into secondary forest or *belukar*.

Employment in agriculture has fallen sharply in the last three decades.In 1960 about 34 per cent of the total working population was in agriculture compared to only 5 per cent in 1981 and about 3 per cent in 1986. Most farms are run by part-time smallholders and wage labour. Farm land is becoming less readily available, especially as some areas of better quality soils have been converted to non-agricultural uses (Wong, 1993). The rigid land purchase and transfer system makes it very difficult to acquire new land for farming purposes. The idling of land resources, the declining self-sufficiency in the major food supplies and the contraction in the major factors of production, namely labour and land, signal clearly the need for a more vigorous diversification programme in the agriculture sector.

Manufacturing industry remains very weakly developed outside the immediate oil-based industries noted in Chapter 3. It contributed only 6.5 per cent to the GDP of Brunei in 1985, and about 4 per cent of total employment through the 1980s. Such data reveals the lack of success in achieving diversification through the expansion of the manufacturing sector. The oil and gas industry remains the dominant manufacturing sector of Brunei, accounting for more than 87 per cent of total manufacturing gross value added in 1983. The non-oil based manufacturing sector today is largely underdeveloped. The government has attempted to promote traditional handicrafts; so far no real success is evident. Efforts to encourage the growth of non-oil based manufacturing industry have been equally unsuccessful: the annual growth rate of this sector was only about 0.5 per cent over the 1974–85 period. It is mainly privately owned and small scale, usually employing fewer than 10 workers, and having paid-up capital of less than B$400,000 (Ministry of Development, 1986). However, the sector accounts for about two-thirds of total employment in the manufacturing sector. In view of its weak performance and its job creation potential, the non-oil based manufacturing sector needs to be given added incentives through the diversification programme.

After community services, construction is the largest service sector employing about 12 per cent of the working population in 1986. Much of that population is however composed of immigrant workers from neighbouring ASEAN countries. It contributed about 2 per cent to GDP through the 1980s. Prior to independence in 1984, the sector was a major source of growth with the expansion in the construction of public buildings but since then the sector has been stagnant. Most construction materials and, as has been noted, labour, are imported; efforts to produce more construction materials locally have been unsuccessful.

5.1.2 The fiscal, investment and banking dimensions

Brunei has huge foreign reserves yet these remain in many respects underutilised. The country's foreign reserves are estimated at about US$30 billion (precise data is not released) and generate a substantial investment income. About forty per cent of the reserves are managed by the Brunei Investment Agency (BIA), and the remainder by foreign institutions (Gunn, 1993, 120). The reserves have been shifted out of sterling stocks (a legacy of the role of the Crown Agents who formerly managed the funds) into more profitable portfolios. A major shortcoming in investment policy is that the utilization of the fund is restrictive and narrowly-based. About 80 per cent of the investments are government bonds, and the rest are cash, equities, gold and real estate (Economist Intelligence Unit, 1990–91). Much of Brunei's excess revenue is banked rather than invested in development, and is held overseas rather than domestically. There is little doubt that if part of such funds were invested in industries that could generate linkages, bring in technology transfer and develop export potentials, the benefits and multipliers to the country would be considerable.

An examination of the sectoral distribution of GDP and employment, together with the investment revenues generated by the hydrocarbon industry, elicits a number of observations about the nature of growth and distribution within the economy. In many respects both the hydrocarbon industry and the revenues it generates remain confined in particular enclaves. Chapter 3 has already suggested the weak links in terms of manufacturing industry between the oil and non-oil sectors. In short there are very few multipliers associated with the oil industry in the economy. The same may apply to the use of investment incomes from oil and gas. These are invested primarily overseas. Furthermore, the revenues which return to the state and population do so largely in terms of a range of 'trickle-down' welfare benefits which, whilst benefiting the local population in a very real sense, do not necessarily generate new income and job-creating industries.

This characteristic is revealed in a number of ways. First, the massive rises in imports (especially of consumer durables) indicates some of the effects of income redistribution in the state. However, investment incomes have not been employed to develop small-scale import-substitution industries which have a ready (and affluent) population to service. Secondly, large quantities of income and profit are repatriated overseas. The state does not impose restrictions on this repatriation either for individuals or companies. Remittances from foreign workers in the state are high and company profits are often repatriated in preference to reinvestment in local companies. In some respects the development potentials of the economy are thwarted by the almost hermetically-sealed nature of the oil industry itself and the revenues generated by that industry.

5.2 EVALUATING THE DIVERSIFICATION STRATEGIES

5.2.1 The promotion of primary resource production

In many countries in Southeast Asia, a profitable and developed agricultural sector has helped to provide commodities for exports or domestic manufacturing industry together with a source of investment funds. Some of the oil-exporting countries in the Middle East such as Saudi Arabia, the United Arab Emirates and Oman have succeeded in generating income from the agricultural sector despite perennial problems of water supply (Azzam, 1988). Glasshouse agriculture and hydroponic farming represent areas of potential growth. In Brunei however, few such linkages are apparent between revenue growth and innovation in farming, hence the clear identification in the development plans of the need to develop the agricultural sector.

Agricultural output can be raised without engendering major structural changes through a range of agronomic techniques such as the greater use of chemical fertilizers and the use of new varieties of high-yielding crops. Brunei has tried to work on such an approach in the past few decades. Government investment in agriculture has been enormous in terms of building up the basic infrastructures, and providing technical and financial assistance. However this strong government support is compromised by the cheap food policies which benefit the population.

Strategies for improving agricultural production and productivity, and diversifying its product base, have been an important component of development plans for at least four decades. The government established programmes for agricultural development in the first, second and third development plans. The targets in the development plans clearly indicated a wish to develop the potential of both non-food and food crops for domestic requirements and export. Expansions in the cultivated area and improvements in yields and quality were anticipated. However no specific targets were set as to the contribution of agriculture to GDP.

In NDP 2, a number of projects were approved in principle but were not given specific budgets and expenditure patterns. The list of projects included irrigation facilities, office buildings for research and training, stores, veterinary clinics, and land settlement schemes. These projects were to provide the supporting framework for wider diversification policies. Tree crops (mainly rubber), together with crops such as jelutong and pepper were also promoted.

In NDP 3, it was clearly stated that the manufacturing sector per se could not provide the framework for diversification without support from agriculture: there 'must be mutual coherence between the development of manufacturing and agriculture, ... and in order to integrate industrialization in the economy, sufficient attention must be paid to agricultural development' (Economic Planning Unit, 1977, p. 44). To accelerate the development of the productive sectors, including both agriculture and manufacturing, NDP 4 spelt out not only the reliance on supportive government polices but also active government participation.

As a result, extensive subsidies and technical assistance were offered to farmers. Modern equipment, high yielding seeds and seedlings, fertilizers and other chemical inputs to promote productivity were given major attention. Research stations were upgraded to provide the necessary guidance and dissemination of the latest technologies. There was also a proposal to strengthen the agricultural resettlement scheme as a follow-up to the training provided in the Sinaut Agricultural Training Centre which was introduced in the third plan. Trainees, after graduation, were expected to become the nucleus of a new generation of commercial farmers in Brunei. NDP 4 also introduced a number of agricultural extension projects to help traditional, subsistence farmers to modernise their holdings.

In the first two plans government participation in the agricultural sector revolved mainly around the construction of basic infrastructural facilities. It also participated directly in a number of rubber plantation schemes such as those in Labi and Temburong. In the third and subsequent plans, the government shifted its attention to projects that met largely local needs. It has allocated resources for the development of large scale rice cultivation and livestock rearing projects with the aim of achieving long-term self-sufficiency. Despite the new emphasis in NDP 3, the investment expenditure allocated for the agriculture sector, including forestry and fisheries, was almost the same as that in the second plan. It formed only about 4.6 per cent ($22.9 million) of the total development allocation. Actual expenditure, however, was $30 million (5.7 per cent of the total). In NDP 4 and NDP 5, the percentage allocated was about 2 per cent ($32 million) and 1.8 per cent respectively. No specific targets were given for the contribution of the agriculture sector to GDP at the end of the respective plan periods. However, in 1979 agriculture contributed 0.65 per cent to GDP; by 1990 the figure had risen to 1.76 per cent.

5.2.2   Basic food crops

To ensure security in the basic food crops, the government set the objective of attaining 30 per cent self-sufficiency in rice production in the fourth and fifth development plans. Between 1978 and 1979, the government approved B\$9.7 million of capital expenditure to develop about 1,000 acres of land at Mulaut and about 5,000 acres at Rambai for rice cultivation. It was estimated that these schemes would produce 10,000 tons of rice per annum which is currently the amount that Brunei imports from Thailand each year. The government also attempted to impose higher prices for locally produced rice as an incentive to local producers. Such an advantage was dampened by the continuing subsidy on imported Thai rice, making it cheaper than the local product and depressing demand. The high costs of production, the shortage of available labour, the limited market size and competition from imported supplies have all combined to make large scale cultivation of rice unfavourable in Brunei. Despite these efforts to encourage rice production, the area and production of rice remains low. The area under rice declined from 2,833 ha in 1962 to only 930 ha in 1989, a graphic illustration of the failure of the 1978/9 schemes. Rice production has also decreased from 5,100 tons in 1962 to only 1,600 tons in 1989. The improvement in yields to an average of 1.68 tons per hectare in 1989 hardly compensates for the fall in production.

Other food crops, mainly vegetables and fruits, have produced rather better results than rice. The area under vegetables has increased from 450 ha in 1984 to 590 ha in 1989 and production of vegetables more than doubled from 640 tons in 1986 to about 1,630 tons in 1989, largely under the impetus of rising urban demand. In general, local production accounted for about 80 per cent of local requirements in the late 1980s. The area under fruit crops almost doubled from 758 ha in 1984 to 1,210 ha in 1989 and production grew from 2,910 tons in 1986 to 3,940 tons in 1989.

5.2.3   Livestock production

Being a Muslim country Brunei primarily consumes chickens, cattle and buffaloes. Pork production, formerly important amongst Chinese smallholders has been phased out by government decree. By the end of 1992, local pork production had disappeared. Production of cattle and buffalo tends to be characterised by poor management, a shortage of good pasture, and dependence on imported feeds. The third plan sought to establish a livestock and meat producing industry based on locally cultivated fodder crops. It was hoped that the state could achieve self-sufficiency in meat and eggs by the early 1980s. That objective has yet to be realised.

In Brunei, cattle and buffalo farming in the private sector is mostly carried out on a smallholder basis. Animals are kept in small herds averaging 4 to 5 animals and are confined to rough grazing around homesteads in the rural areas and in abandoned rice fields. The total area of open, grass covered swamplands that are used as grazing lands is approximately 7,000 ha. The average size of grazing land used per smallholder was about 7.5 ha. These extensive methods of livestock rearing contribute to the low productivity in the country. In view of the poor performance of the private sector in livestock farming, the government has sought to improve productivity and pasturing through advice and direct participation. The task of improving the local breeds is entrusted to the research stations of the Department of Agriculture, the Buffalo Breeding Farm in Kiudang in Tutong district, the Luahan Cattle Breeding Station and Jerudong Cattle Fattening Station. These stations have attempted to improve the local breed by crossing it with imported foreign breeds. The first consignment of buffaloes to stock the farms was imported from Australia and stall fed at the Jerudong Cattle Fattening Station before being moved in 1986.

Direct participation in livestock farming has come through the McFarm cattle farming enterprise in Brunei, a joint venture between the government and the Mitsubishi Corporation of Japan. It covers an area of 485 ha and is located north of Bandar Seri Begawan near Tungku, Mukim Gadong. It was started in 1978. In 1979 breeding herds were imported from Australia, an area of about 180 ha was cleared and roughly 120 ha planted to improved pastures. Operations began with a herd of about 740 head. The farm is heavily overstocked due to the current inability to sell off young breeding stock and young steers for fattening. The objective of the farm was to produce young animals for building up smallholder herds. The response, however, was poor despite government attempts to stimulate demand by reducing the price to be paid to McFarm for their young stock. Consequently, McFarm has been unable to dispose of its surplus stock and is forced to purchase additional feed for its animals as well as sell the mature stock.

Besides direct government participation, cattle rearing is encouraged through the Young Farmers Settlement Schemes. Between 1976 and 1983 about 100 young local men were trained at the Sinaut Agricultural Training Centre to become full-time commercial farmers. After finishing the two-year course, these trainees were given help in establishing small farms in selected settlement areas. Several of these farms included a cattle fattening unit, consisting of some steers obtained from local breeding herds at McFarm and the Department's Luahan Cattle Breeding Station. The plan has failed for several reasons. The farm sites were unsuitable for the production of fodder and farmers were not accustomed to hand feeding the animals regularly. The prices paid for the live animals (B$3.35 per kg) were also considered too low due to competition from imported beef (Ministry of Development, 1986). As a result, most of the young farmers have now abandoned their livestock enterprises or changed over to poultry production. In addition to promoting and expanding local production, the government has invested in foreign farms to ensure constant beef supply for the State. The Government acquired a 2,226 sq mile cattle and buffalo ranch in Willerroo in the Northern Territory of Australia in 1981.

Despite government support and promotion, local production of beef actually declined slightly from 253 tons in 1977 to 223 tons in 1984. The number of both cattle and buffaloes has been decreasing steadily. Cattle numbers fell from 3,277 in 1960 to 2,000 head in 1985 for cattle, and from 14,430 heads to 5,000 heads in 1985 for buffaloes. Since 1985 there have been some increases in production with the weight of local cattle slaughtered rising by around 30 per cent. However, local production is outstripped by beef imports which tripled between 1960 and 1985. About one third of these imports came from Australia, another third from south America and about 20 per cent from Malaysia. Local beef supplied only about 10 per cent of local demand in the late 1980s.

Whilst the cattle farming projects have not achieved the targets envisaged in the development plans, some success is evident for smaller livestock. Commercial production of poultry is centred in Bandar Seri Begawan, where 72 per cent of the total production is concentrated. Seria and Kuala Belait are the other important centres. Poultry production in Brunei has emerged from the traditional backyard production to modern, large scale commercial enterprises. Broiler production showed a steady increase from 2,045 tons in 1977 to 4,000 tons in 1984 before falling back somewhat to around 2,800 tons in 1989. Imports of poultry products have decreased considerably since the late 1970s. In 1990, 2.27 million broilers and 3,412 tons of dressed poultry meat were produced; this local production from both commercial and homestead farms can now satisfy about 87 per cent of the total consumption of broiler chickens in the country. About half of the broiler chickens are produced in Brunei-Muara district with Tutong and Belait producing one-quarter each.

Government assistance and support has clearly been of major importance in the success of poultry production in meeting local demand. Government promotion of the poultry industry dates from NDP 2. In 1967 a poultry subsidy scheme was implemented in which farmers were given 50 chicks and feed mash sufficient for four months. The scheme laid the foundations for a major expansion in this sector. The expansion of the poultry sector can also be attributed to the less demanding conditions required. Some of the farmers on the Young Farmers Settlement Schemes changed from cattle fattening to broiler production, but the scale of their enterprises is comparatively small. To reduce competition from imported products, the import of live table birds was stopped in 1968 but the dependence on imported chicks remains. At present about 2 million day-old chicks are imported per year, mainly from Singapore. About 480,000 chicks are produced locally per year, accounting for about 18 per cent of total day old chicks used for production. Efforts to develop egg production in the state have also been successful; 21 commercial production units located in the main population centres have been established. In 1969 about 50 per cent of local consumption was imported from Sarawak and Singapore. By 1990, local production accounted for 97 per cent of domestic needs. To reduce competition with imported eggs, an import quota of about 3.5 per cent of the total requirements was set in 1990.

5.2.4   Agricultural training

Besides the provision of loans and subsidies, and the expansion of agricultural and horticultural research facilities, the government, with the financial and technical help of Brunei Shell, established the Sinaut Agricultural Training Centre in the mid-1970s. In 1990 there were almost 100 students enrolled for a range of diplomas in agriculture and agricultural engineering. The intention underlying the creation of the programmes was to help provide graduates with the skills to move into agriculture. This has not always been the case and many graduates have sought and gained work outside farming (Wong, 1993). The gap between remuneration in farming and in the public sector remains a major barrier to greater involvement of the citizen population in agricultural production.

5.2.5 Fisheries

To promote the development of fishery resources, a number of potential estuarine and coastal areas have been identified for shrimp, prawn and fish culture; as Selvanathan Subramaniam (1992) has noted, the long tradition of fishing in the state gives it the potential to expand in a managed and scientific manner. The government has made major efforts to provide supportive facilities such as the construction of ice breaking plants and landing platforms. A hatchery, fish ponds and training unit have been eŝtablished for promoting aquaculture and offshore marine fisheries. The formation of fishing cooperatives has also been effective and successful. Loans are given for the purchase of fishing gear, boats and other necessities. However the lack of local expertise in the control of water quality and fishery management and labour shortages have prevented large-scale commercial operations. Thus the commercial prawn farm started in 1979 on the 1,000 acre site at Biang on Temburong River was a commercial failure. Overall the quantity of fresh fish products produced in Brunei has reduced by one-quarter from 2.1 million kgs in 1975 to 1.8 million kgs in 1990 whilst imports almost trebled from about 1.3 million kgs to 3.7 million kgs over the same period.

5.3 PROMOTING THE MANUFACTURING SECTOR

In all the development plans, the parallel restructuring of both industry and agriculture has been seen as the preferred means of correcting the imbalances of the economy. Yet such rhetoric is often at odds with the actual budgetary committments to such policy. Thus in NDP 3 the allocation of actual development expenditure to industry formed only 0.1 per cent ($760,000) compared to the expected 1.8 per cent ($9 million) of the total. In NDP 4, instead of $4 million, only $833,000 was spent. In NDP 5 a sum of $373 million or 10 per cent of total was allocated to industry and commerce, 5 per cent of which was to be used for industrial promotion. The government's role has been centred on the provision of basic infrastructural facilities and a range of fiscal incentives. In the case of manufacturing industry it primarily involves the setting up of industrial estates; the government has not sought direct participation (through for example joint ventures) in the manufacturing sector. The major types of industries that have been suggested for private investment are forestry-based industries, non-oil mineral based industries and agro-industrial enterprises.

The NDP 5 elaborated on some of the constraints faced by manufacturing industry and suggested a number of areas where action was needed. These included: a review of the land code, policies to nurture a class of Malay entrepreneurs (an imitation of the New Economic Policy of Malaysia), the establishment of a development bank, the setting up of a national pension scheme or employee provident fund, and the implementation of a national training scheme. Other suggestions mooted included the privatisation of some government services, the establishment of public enterprises through direct participation or joint ventures and the provision of a range of incentives for private sector development. Without specifying particular industries, it has been suggested that the government will participate actively in high risk areas.

5.3.1   Government incentives for the manufacturing sector

The onus for overseeing and monitoring the process and progress of industrial diversification rests with the Economic Development Board which was modelled on the equivalent Singapore board (Chi, 1991). To promote the manufacturing sector as a means of economic diversification, a range of incentives has been introduced to encourage participation from the private sector, both foreign and domestic. These incentives include tax-holidays for firms granted pioneer status. A firm can be given pioneer status if it engages in an industry previously not carried out in the country on a commercial scale. The industry must be suited to the economic and development needs of the nation, and there should be favourable prospects for further developing the industry to provide for exports. Pioneer status is also given if there are insufficient facilities in the country to carry out the industry on a commercial scale and it is in the public interest.

Tax exemption is given to a pioneer company from the date it commences production on a scale which increases with the size of its fixed capital investments. The tax exemption period is two years for fixed capital investment of up to $250,000, three years for over $250,000–$500,000, four years for over $500,000–$1 million and five years for over $1 million. It is also exempted from customs duty on items to be installed in the factory and from paying import duties on raw materials not available in Brunei. Incentives are also given to established companies which intend to expand and incur new capital expenditure. The tax relief period for an expanded enterprise is three years for new capital expenditure of less than $250,000 and five years for more than $250,000. To facilitate the access to capital loans, tax relief on interest paid to non-resident lenders is provided for pioneer industries. The government may also grant tax exemption for any approved foreign loan if the loan is used for the purchase of productive equipment and the amount of the loan is at least $200,000.

A range of industries have been granted pioneer status (Table 5.3). These include aircraft catering services, cement production, pharmaceuticals, aluminium production, ceramics and rolling mill plants which manufacture iron and steel, steel bars and angle irons. Industrial chemicals for the oil and other industries are also given pioneer status; these include the manufacture of corrosion inhibitors, bactericides, demulsifiers, gas inhibitors, oxygen scavengers and detergents manufactured or blended in Brunei. Ship repair and maintenance has also been allocated pioneer status. Industries that produce basic consumer goods not

Table 5.3   Pioneer status industries, 1991

Industries	Products
Aircraft catering	Food for airlines
Cement finish mill	Cement
Pharmaceutical	Medicines; vitamins
Aluminium tiles	Wall tiles; decorative tiles
Rolling mill plant	Iron and steel; bars; angle irons
Industrial chemicals	Chemicals for the oil industry; bactericides;
Shipyard	Ship repair and maintenance
Paper	Tissue paper; napkins
Textiles	Garment manufacture
Canning, bottling	Canned soft drinks; packaged food, mineral waters

Source: Economic Development Board, 1991.

produced in Brunei (paper tissues, textiles, canning and bottling) are also listed.

There is no capital gains tax in Brunei. However companies are subject to tax on gains or profits from any trade, business or vocation, on dividends received from companies not previously assessed for tax in the state, on interest and discounts and rents, royalties, premiums, and on any other profits arising from properties. However all expenses incurred in the production of taxable income are deductible for tax purposes. These include interest on borrowed money used in acquiring income, rent on land and building used in the trade or business, costs of repair of premises, plant and machinery, bad debts and employers' contributions to approved pension or provident funds. Other fiscal incentives have been included in the programme. Basic foodstuffs and goods for industrial use are exempted from import duties. Electrical equipment and appliances, timber products, photographic materials and equipment, furniture, motor vehicles and spare parts attract duties of 20 per cent. Cosmetics and perfumes are subject to 30 per cent duty. The rates for other dutiable items are low compared with neighbouring countries. There are no export, sales, payroll or manufacturing taxes in the state.

These fiscal benefits cannot however be fully utilized and in some ways are irrelevant to the contemporary structure of manufacturing industry. Most manufacturing industry is small-scale and oriented towards the domestic market. A government survey commissioned in 1987 revealed that about 90 per cent of domestic manufacturing production was absorbed by the domestic market. There was some exporting of furniture, bricks and tiles to Sabah but the amount was small. A similar pattern prevailed for the limited exports to Sarawak. The small domestic market and small scale of operation limits the demand for raw materials; it is therefore not surprising that about 77 per cent of the industrial establishments in Brunei obtained more than half of their raw materials from within the country (Ministry of Development, 1986).

Besides a range of fiscal incentives, the government has built up the physical infrastructure to give a stronger push to the industrial programme. A number of industrial estates have been established as potential growth centers for industrial development in both light and heavy industrial products (Figure 5.1). These include the Brunei–Muara Industrial Estate consisting of the Bandar Seri Begawan and Muara Industrial Estates, the Belait Industrial Estate consisting of Seria and Kuala Belait Industrial Estates, the Tutong Industrial Area and the

111

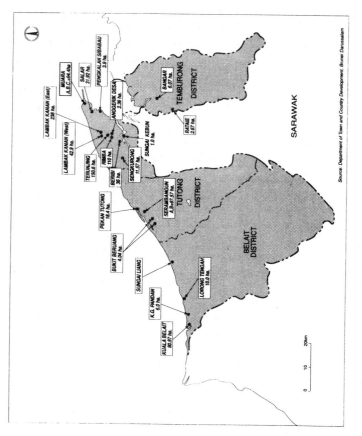

Figure 5.1   Industrial estates in Brunei, 1990

LAMBAK KANAN (East)
238 ha.

MUARA
A.B.C.=44.4ha

SALAR
31.92 ha.

PENGKALAN SIBABAU
3.9 ha.

LAMBAK KANAN (West)
42.9 ha.

ANGGERIK DESA
2.36 ha.

BANGAR
6.07 ha.

TERUNJONG
150.6 ha.

RIMBA
110 ha.

BERIBI
36 ha.

SENGKURONG
11.57 ha.

SUNGAI KEBUN
1.0 ha.

RATAIE
2.57 ha.

TEMBURONG
DISTRICT

SERAMBANGUN
A.B=7.57 ha.

TUTONG
DISTRICT

SARAWAK

PEKAN TUTONG
18.4 ha.

BUKIT BERUANG
4.04 ha.

SUNGAI LIANG

LORONG TENGAH
10.0 ha.

BELAIT
DISTRICT

K.G. PANDAN
6.0 ha.

KUALA BELAIT
80.97 ha.

0   10   20km

Source: Department of Town and Country Development, Brunei Darussalam

Temburong Industrial Area (Chi, 1991). The response from the private sector in locating their industries in these estates has not been encouraging, and only the estates in the capital have attracted solid numbers of enterprises.

Three-fifths of the non-oil based manufacturing industries takes place in the most populous district, the Brunei–Muara district. Industries such as baking, beverages, clothing, furniture making, printing/publishing and brick-making are mostly located in the capital, and the oil centres, Seria and Kuala Belait. Many do not favour location in the industrial estates. The majority of the industrial establishments of non-oil based industries are located in either detached factories or shophouses. Industries such as metal products, brick, pottery and tile making, furniture, sawmilling and miscellaneous industry indicate a clear preference for detached factories. The food processing establishments are mostly located in shophouses. Sawmilling and furniture-making tend to be dispersed in the Belait, Tutong and Temburong district, rather than in the industrial estates. Owing to land acquisition problems, most of the industrial establishments are found in rented premises. Government surveys indicate that only about 15 per cent are on owned land while only 3 per cent are located in industrial estates (Ministry of Development, 1986) All printing and publishing firms are operating on rented premises. The non-oil based industries are labour-intensive; however, as Arief (1986, 91–2) notes, immigrant workers accounted for as much as 60 per cent of the workforce employed in that sector in the early 1980s.

A number of administrative reforms have been implemented to upgrade the role of the industrial programme. A new ministry, the Ministry of Industry and Primary Resources was established on 1st January 1989. Its responsibility is to promote and encourage the development of productive industrial activities. It also has the task of coordinating industrial development activities. It has established a 'one-stop agency' as the focal point for all industrial development enquiries and applications.

Overall, then, industrial policy centers around the provision of fiscal incentives and physical infrastructures for promoting industrial development. Other more important and pragmatic factors are rarely discussed in detail such as industrial land purchase and transfer, bureaucratic delays over labour quotas or payment, the period of lease, equity ownership, manpower training and the development of linkages with interrelated industries. As a result, many existing firms are still having difficulties running their businesses. The pattern of non-oil based manufacturing industry in Brunei thus remains essentially simple and underdeveloped. Only the next decade will determine whether the policies of the last two or three years will instigate a radical change to this pattern. Despite the rhetoric and policies of the last three development plans, the country has by far the least diversified manufacturing structures among the ASEAN countries. After many years of policies designed to develop the manufacturing sector, Brunei remains handicapped by the shortage of labour, entrepreneurial and management skills and technical expertise, the small domestic market and the lack of good networks with foreign markets.

5.4 PROMOTING THE FINANCIAL SECTOR

Unlike some other small, oil-rich countries such as Bahrain (Nugent and Thomas, 1985), Brunei has not used its enormous reserves and revenues to develop as a regional financial centre. Its financial investments in the international market were small until the oil-price boom of the 1970s. As part of the programme of diversification, these investments can be used productively in at least three ways. A first way is to build up a strong financial sector at home that is supported by both domestic and foreign resources. Secondly, increased domestic financial resources may help to develop an expertise in banking and financial transactions based on Islamic principles. A third element would be to diversify the use and regional location of overseas investments.

The intention to turn Brunei into a regional financial centre reflects an attempt to maximize the use of its domestic financial resources. The rise in oil prices has made Brunei extraordinarily rich in capital and there are substantial surpluses which can be used for investments in the country. Thus improvements to the financial sector are important not only to assist investment and development, but also to generate wealth within the country as well as recycle funds abroad. Preparing Brunei for a role as a regional financial centre in the future was mooted in NDP 5. Besides helping to diversify the economy, the move was seen as meeting the rising needs of the private sector, both foreign and local, for investment in local industries. The absence of strong controls on financial transactions are listed as incentives for further development of this sector; there are, for example, no restrictions on importing capital from any country, or on overseas remittances of capital or profits. Non-resident accounts can be maintained and there is no restriction on borrowing by non-residents. The currency is at par with that of Singapore and interest rates tend to move in line with those of Singapore. Planners hope that this liberal system and free flow of funds can help establish Brunei as a favourable haven for offshore capital investment.

Banking regulation in Brunei is founded on British law and the earliest banks, the Hongkong and Shanghai Banking Corporation and Standard Chartered Bank were established in the late-1940s with the support of the British administration. Government funds were the major source of revenue given the small deposit base in the state. Malayan Banking (1960) was the first 'non-colonial' bank to be licenced; it was followed by the United Malayan Banking Corporation (1963), the National Bank of Brunei (1964) and Citibank (1971). The Island Development Bank (1980) was the last to be licensed. Licence fees and corporate tax are low and, at times, banking activity has been poorly scrutinised.

Direct deposits are the primary source of funds; both Citibank and Hongkong Bank had deposits of over one billion dollars in late-1989, with Standard Chartered about half-a-billion. It was estimated in late-1989 that around 80 per cent of the total deposit base was placed offshore by Brunei's banks, most being transferred to the head offices of the major banks. 'Officials', noted one report, 'are increasingly concerned over the banks using the country as a source of relatively cheap funds which can be more profitably loaned offshore' (ASEAN, 1991, 17–18). Most of the funds are directed to Singapore, thus avoiding any exchange rate fluctuations. Those funds that are invested locally focus on three areas: personal loans, construction and general commerce. In 1989 only $12 million out of total domestic lending of $967 million was directed to investment in manufacturing.

The financial infrastructures of the state are relatively restricted. Recent growth in the level of resources handled by banks has meant that reforms of regulations have been mooted as a means of matching financial resources to the development needs of the state. Because of the Islamic prohibition on interest, many depositors pay little attention to interest rates, which are often very low. The interest rates charged on local loans more often reflect Singapore rates rather than local ones; in short, business borrowers often pay more for their capital than local conditions would otherwise dictate. Singapore, unlike Brunei, protects itself against such trends by ruling that local deposits can only be used for operations within Singapore. As one recent report argued, 'there is every reason to believe that the level of industrial and commercial development in Brunei Darussalam would be greatly enhanced if the internal supply of funds were a greater determinant of the interest rates' (ASEAN, 1991, 40).

The idea of turning Brunei into a regional financial centre was conceived in the mid-1980s. In July 1985, the Sultan secured a 51 per cent stake in the Island Development Bank (IDB). The bank's chairman, a Filipino entrepreneur, Enrique Zobel held 29 per cent and Japan's Dai Ichi Kangyo Bank took the remaining 20 per cent. In 1984 Zobel suggested making IDB the main development bank of Brunei and eventually the biggest in the region. Before the idea was crystalised, a scandal in connection with the now defunct National Bank of Brunei (NBB) was discovered. In 1986 the government seized the assets of the bank having discovered its conspiracy to defraud the assets of the bank. Until 1986 NBB was the second largest local bank and 70 per cent of its equity was owned by the Sultan. With the closure of the NBB, the IDB became the only local bank in Brunei and was renamed the International Bank of Brunei (IBB). The founding chairman resigned and the Deputy Director of the Economic Development Board became the director of the bank. The bank will concentrate on expanding its foreign business. The development bank functions will be taken over by a state agency.

In the process of diversifying out of sterling investments, and as part of the decision to remove most of the investment portfolios from the British Crown Agents, the Brunei Investment Agency was set up in 1983. In view of the time consuming process of training local staff, and the immediate shortage of skills and expertise, four agencies including Morgan Guarantee Trust and City Bank from the United States together with the Nomura and Daiwa Securities of Japan became the major investment consultants to Brunei. These firms, except Morgan Guarantee, were also the portfolio advisers stationed in Brunei to undertake the training of local staff. In addition BIA has opened offices in London and New York. Since the establishment of the BIA, investment performance has sharply improved. The country's foreign investments are now widely spread out in the Asia Pacific region and cater to the needs of the nation. Some examples are the investment in the hotel industry of Singapore, the investment in the Australian Willerroo ranch to ensure adequate beef supplies, and the investment in the Indonesian cement industry to help counteract the shortage of cement and other construction materials in Brunei.

Most observers are sceptical of Brunei's future as a financial centre for the region owing to its lack of financial expertise and a consequent inability to compete with other highly sophisticated centres in the Asia-Pacific region such as Tokyo, Hong Kong and Singapore. In addition, Malaysia's intention to establish Labuan as an offshore investment centre will almost certainly compromise Brunei's efforts in this area. The expansion potential of foreign banks in Brunei remains constrained by the small domestic market and by a lack of demand for traditional banking services, owing to state provision of loans for the purchase of houses and cars by government officers, and to a shortage of trained and experienced banking staff and financial experts. Nevertheless, the country's vast national reserves, growing local expertise within the BIA, and the developing financial links established by the major holding company in the country, QAF Holdings, offers some potential for Brunei's development as a merchant banking centre in the region. In the short term, however, real progress appears unlikely.

5.5 THE PROSPECTS FOR DIVERSIFICATION

The many attempts to diversify the national economy have met with some success, albeit limited. Perhaps more importantly, they have served to identify the magnitude of the task facing development planners. In future a number of problems will continue to constrain the further diversification of the economy.

5.5.1 Labour, production and investment constraints

In promoting the agriculture and manufacturing sectors as a means of diversification, the gap in wage levels between the two sectors and, in particular, between the public and oil sectors, and the rest of the economy has been a central problem. In 1981 the real annual wages of workers in non-oil based manufacturing industry were $5,403 compared to the average annual income of about $11,000 that prevailed in the rest of the economy (1981 Population Census). Whilst the full results of the 1990 Census are not yet available, it is expected that this wage-gap will remain. These differences are a disincentive to the movement of labour to the non-oil manufacturing sector, and reflects one of the manifestations of the 'Dutch Disease' discussed in Chapter 4. In addition to higher wages the public sector includes generous fringe benefits such as education allowances, subsidised housing, housing loans. at negative real interest rates and interest free car loans. These factors, argues Colclough (1985, 31), 'lead to a remuneration structure which cannot be replicated by those industries which have to compete on the international market with products from countries where labour costs may be very low'. Besides having lower wage levels, the non-oil sector has exhibited declining labour productivity. The gross value-added per worker declined by 6 per cent between 1974 and 1981 and by 8.8 per cent between 1981 and 1985 (Ministry of Development, 1986). The low level of labour productivity in non-oil based manufacturing reflects the predominance of small, individually owned units and the associated problems of gaining scale economies.

It may be argued that the labour question is at the heart of the success of the diversification programme. Labour is both costly and often characterised by low productivity. In addition there is a problem of labour shortage. This labour shortage has been offset to a limited extent by a steady rise in the participation of females in the labour force, an important achievement given the dominance of Islam in the country. However, the labour shortage problem remains. A numerical shortage is further compounded by shortages of skilled labour; many unemployed do not have the necessary technical, clerical or administrative skills required by the private sector. This is reflected in vacancy levels; a survey in late-1989 showed that of 299 vacancies in the public sector in 1989, only about one-third were filled. For the private sector only one-sixth of vacancies were filled (*Borneo Bulletin* 10/2/90).

A large proportion of the local labour force is unskilled. Unskilled workers constituted about 82 per cent of Brunei's total labour force in the early-1980s (Brunei Labour Department Survey, 1983). The country is heavily reliant on foreign labour in professional and technical occupations as well as unskilled areas. In 1989 there were almost 26,000 foreign workers in the state, almost one-third of the workforce (Economic Planning Unit, 1990). What little industrial development that has occurred has relied heavily on labour imported from other countries in Southeast or South Asia. Foreign labour is imported to staff both the private and public sectors; Brunei has low comparative advantages in labour cost and characteristics compared to its ASEAN neighbours.

Attempts to overcome the skills problem of the labour force have been a part of the recent expansion of tertiary education in the country.

Prior to the establishment of Universiti Brunei Darussalam in 1985, tertiary students were educated abroad, primarily in the United Kingdom, with the aid of generous government grants. The creation of the university has undoubtedly increased the numbers of graduates, although the liberal-arts tradition within which many courses at the university have been framed has meant that students are perhaps best suited to public sector employment. Early graduates in the Malay medium have found difficulties in gaining employment leading to a renewed emphasis on English language instruction. The bulk of the graduates are destined for teaching posts. Formal vocational training has been expanded with the creation of the Institute of Technology designed to produce graduates for a changing job market with clear technical skills that can be applied in the industrial sector. As yet, the results have been equivocal with around 60 per cent of graduates in 1990 being in the general arts category: the education system, it has been suggested, 'is suffering from a severe qualitative malaise in the midst of material luxury' (Attwood and Bray, 1989, 74).

In some areas increased government action can help to mitigate some of the labour difficulties. In particular, projects to make the private sector more attractive are needed. Whilst government sector wages have been static since 1986, the range of broader fringe benefits still make the public sector more attractive. Attempts to introduce a national pension scheme for private sector workers have not yet passed beyond the drawing board. A more radical option, the axing of some of the benefits and welfare schemes provided in the public sector, has yet to be proposed. Such a policy may invite dissent and political opposition in the short-run. It might be argued that without the political will to make the structural shift in the effective distribution of labour, the diversification programme is unlikely to succeed.

A second impediment to diversification is the problem of land acquisition and ownership. Most land belongs to the state and is rented only with temporary occupation licences. Thus incentives for investment in land for farming or industry are limited. Long-term investments which require substantial amount of capital such as machinery and equipment are unattractive given that most land is available only on one-year leases.

Supply input constraints are a third factor limiting the diversification programme. Whilst Brunei's utilities are competitively priced and both ground rents and interest rates on government soft loans are relatively low in regional terms, the country produces few of the raw materials and intermediate industrial products needed for a major diversification drive. Not only does a reliance on imports result in higher input prices, it also creates additional risk through the uncertainty of supply. A recent survey has shown that shortages of machinery and equipment are major problems amongst local manufacturing concerns together with a lack of capital (Wimalatissa, 1992, 227).

A fourth constraint on diversification is the chronic concentration of domestic private investment in the oil sector. In 1975 about 80 per cent of total development investment came from the private sector; out of that figure, 80 per cent went into the oil sector. In the late 1970s and early 1980s as much as 90 per cent of private sector investment was concentrated in the oil sector. In 1985 the oil sector still absorbed about 60 per cent of all investment although, as in the earlier period, a higher proportion of private investment remained in that sector (Table 5.4). This bias in private investment towards the oil sector has had serious consequences for investment patterns in the non-oil sector. Thus between 1975 and 1980 investment in the oil sector grew by about 15 per cent a year while the non-oil sector experienced a decline of 1.7 per cent. As Table 5.5 indicates, between 1980 and 1985 private sector investment fell by 7.1 per cent, largely due to the decline in oil prices (Moehammad Nazir, 1992, 209). According to the Fifth Plan the bulk of private investment in the plan period will continue to be in the oil sector.

Table 5.4   Public and private sector investment, 1975–85

Year	Govt (a)	Private (b)	Oil as % b	Total ($m)	Invest. as %GDP
1975	17.2	82.8	82.4	514	0.19
1976	23.2	76.8	90.9	498	0.14
1977	16.2	83.8	92.6	537	0.13
1978	16.4	83.6	90.8	511	0.12
1979	23.7	76.3	91.2	671	0.11
1980	18.8	81.2	90.9	935	0.09
1981	15.7	84.3	93.6	1398	0.15
1982	24.1	75.9	92.9	1566	0.17
1983	35.3	64.7	89.7	1347	0.17
1984	35.2	64.8	84.7	971	0.12
1985	38.8	61.2	80.5	856	0.11

Source: Brunei Statistical Yearbooks; NDP 5 (1986–90).

Table 5.5   Annual growth of investment (%), 1975–85

Years	Govt	Private	Oil	Non-oil	Total
1975–80	14.8	12.3	14.5	−1.7	12.7
1980–85	13.5	−7.1	−9.4	8.2	−1.7
1975–85	14.2	2.1	1.9	3.1	5.2

Source: NDP 5 (1986–90).

The share of government investment in generating economic growth has increased steadily. In 1975 about 17 per cent of total investment came from the government; by 1983 its share had grown to 35 per cent (Table 5.4). At the end of NDP 4 it was close to 40 per cent. The increased dependence on government investment hardly creates the best environment for diversification which, as NDP 5 noted, requires much greater private investment activity.

5.5.2   Finance and investment capital

A particular enterpreneurial problem has, rather ironically in this rich country, been an inability to tap both local and external sources of finance. The banks and financial institutions usually require land title documents as collateral for a loan. The problem of land acquisition not only weakens the incentive to participate in diversification, but also compounds the problem of access to financial loans. To overcome this constraint, Islamic banking systems are beginning to emerge in order to pool the domestic financial resources of a largely Muslim population. The Brunei Islamic Trust Fund (TAIB or Tabung Amanah Islam Brunei) was launched personally by the Sultan in September 1991. The objectives are to manage a fund with the same name, and eventually sponsor investment and trade including investments in the stock and financial markets and participation in industrial and economic developments at home. The Fund will operate through a financial savings system whereby investments will be made and dividends paid on a profit basis after deducting payment for the *zakat* tithe and the cost of management. It was disclosed by the Sultan that the International Bank of Brunei will become the nucleus for the first Islamic bank in the country (*Brunei Darussalam Newsletter*, Feb. 1992).

Currently a vast amount of the financial capital in Brunei is spent on the extension of welfare services and on personal consumption. If the diversification policy is to be successful increased attention is required to ensure that capital is shifted into income-generating and job-creating industries and services in the private sector. Public sector spending will have to be increasingly evaluated in terms of its effectiveness in assisting the private sector and in pursuing the objectives of diversification.

Much of Brunei's finance and investment capital continues to be invested overseas. One of the most important agencies has been QAF Holdings which was established in 1982. It is 65 per cent owned by the foreign minister, who is one of the Sultan's brothers. QAF became a public company in 1984. It has expanded rapidly, setting up interests in food trading and processing, the offshore oil industry, and ventures ranging from newspapers to air conditioners. It has also established a Malaysian subsidiary which operates a supermarket and warehouse business. It has been involved in offshore drilling in Panama as well as in Brunei through joint venture partnership with foreign companies such as Reading and Bates. In 1984, QAF acquired 65 per cent of Ben and Company, a subsidiary of Straits Steamship, and gained a listing on the Singapore Stock Exchange. In 1985 it bought a 60 per cent share in a joint venture with Singapore's Emporium Holdings, which operates the largest chain of supermarkets and department stores in Singapore. Since then, the expansion of QAF through acquisitions has continued. In 1986 it was disclosed that QAF was to pay B$2.25 million for the technological assets of Vosper Pte. Ltd, a Singapore based shipbuilding company which was in liquidation. At the same time, QAF's wholly owned Australian subsidiary Spices of the Orient (Soto) was reported to have acquired another company, Hemphill's Herbs and Spices Pte Ltd. QAF is at present the third largest employer in Brunei after the public sector and Brunei Shell. Recently, QAF has begun expanding into China and Myanmar; net profits of the group doubled in 1992.

In addition Bruneian companies are beginning to focus on investment opportunities in Indochina. The establishment of diplomatic links with Vietnam has encouraged investment there. The recent investment by a Bruneian company, Primal Corporation, headed by Prince Sufri Bolkiah, of some $9 billion over a 20-year period, exemplifies the trend of overseas rather than domestic investment. It also underlines the close nexus between companies with strong royal connections, the Brunei Investment Agency and state investment decisions. Investment in oil and gas has continued unabated. In 1991, Brunei LNG awarded a US$120 million contract to build two new LNG storage tanks to a consortium of Japanese (Toyo Kanetsu) and German manufacturers. It is to be carried out jointly with a local partner, Paja Sdn Bhd. For completion in 1994, the tanks will each have a capacity of 65,000 cu m. Brunei LNG's existing storage tanks were built twenty years ago.

As was noted earlier, the prospects for expanding the financial sector are constrained by the fact that the local banks suffer from the lack of a local deposit base. The government and Brunei Shell deposit their funds in the three major banks, namely Hongkong and Shanghai Banking Corporation, the Chartered Bank and the International Bank of Brunei. The normal bank business of the government and Brunei Shell has been traditionally shared with the three banks to meet their own operational requirements and for investment purposes. These three have most access to the government's funds and have developed branch systems within the country. But the government and Brunei Shell can control the money supply through regulating its expenditures, and deciding whether to take payment of the royalties and dividends from Shell abroad or in Brunei. The small banks must therefore attract the big local depositors away from the other banks or borrow on the Singapore interbank market in order to fund their local lending, incurring higher cost of funds than the three major banks.

The parity between the Brunei and Singapore dollar has no doubt cut the cost of transactions for the government but it has created an undesirable impact. Parity discourages the interbank market in Brunei since the larger banks are able to redeposit their surplus funds in Singapore, and prefer to do so rather than lend locally to their competitors. The smaller banks, with an insufficient Brunei dollar deposit base, are thus forced to borrow on the Singapore market to finance local lending. The larger local customers generally have good business connections in Singapore and will borrow or deposit their funds directly in Singapore if the rates between the two markets differ greatly. As a result there is a substantial flow of investment monies from Brunei to the offshore financial markets, notably Hongkong and Singapore.

The government also intervenes directly in the financial market. The Economic Development Board (EDB), Treasury Department and the Resettlement Department all loan to the private sector. The EDB has made loans for small and medium businesses since 1977 at a rate of 6 per cent on the reducing monthly balance for periods as long as ten years. A large part of the budgeted loan balance is however not made because of bureaucratic delays. The Treasury Department provides interest free car loans and housing loans for government officers at up to three times annual salary levels at fixed rates of 0.5 per cent. The Resettlement Department provides land and houses for residents with twenty-year interest-free mortgages. The intervention of the government in these areas further reduces the scope for a more diverse Brunei banking system.

Brunei clearly faces major problems in implementing the diversification strategy. However they are far from insuperable if the political will and committment is manifest. The population is young, literate and increasingly well-educated. The country has an abundance of capital which provides a framework for both secure investment revenues and growth in the domestic economy. Furthermore the country is located in a region with some of the highest growth rates in the world.

As this chapter has argued, the rhetoric of development and diversification has been a constant element for at least two decades yet the achievements have been modest, to say the least. Building a more diverse economy requires programmes to overcome a series of constraints — labour, capital, resources and management skills — which are not unique to Brunei, but which take on a particular force given the small size and unbalanced economy of the state. Given concerns about rising domestic unemployment within the context of a political and cultural system that is often highly rigid, conservative and traditionalist, the success of the diversification strategy may well be a key element in the future political and social stability of the state. It is to those interrelationships in both the national and international context that Chapter 6 turns.

6 The Political Economy of Oil

The nature and progress of development planning in the state has been of considerable significance in shaping the evolving political economy of Brunei both domestically and in the international context. Oil and gas — its production, processing, role in the generation of income and wealth and concomitant international linkages — have been fundamental in shaping the political development of the state and securing its future. Domestic and foreign policy in Brunei has both shaped and reflected the changing economic and political position of the country since the first oil price rise and the achievement of independence.

6.1 POLITICAL STRUCTURES AND INSTITUTIONS

The most important institution in Brunei is the ruling family itself, led by the Sultan. The political, economic and social position of the Royal Family is paramount in Brunei; the appointment by the Sultan of two of his brothers as Ministers of Finance and Foreign Affairs has reinforced this. The present ruling family is descended from Omar Ali Saifuddin 1 who ruled from 1750–80. The father of the present Sultan, Omar Ali Saifuddin III abdicated in favour of Hassanal Bolkiah in 1967. He died in 1986. The system of succession to the throne of Brunei was not stabilised until the early part of the twentieth century. No one may succeed without the consent of the Council of Succession which consists of the nobility and other high officials. The social system of the country is highly structured and rank and protocol are central (Brown, 1970). Ranking beneath the Sultan are the members of the ruling family, the *wazirs* of noble descent, the non-noble officials and the commoners (Figure 6.1).

As was noted in Chapter 2, the political system in the country is that of a Malay Muslim Monarchy. Democratic government, as understood in the West, is of a different nature in Brunei. Attempts to establish a degree of parliamentary democracy, pursued in the late 1950s and early 1960s, foundered during the 1962 emergency and have not been

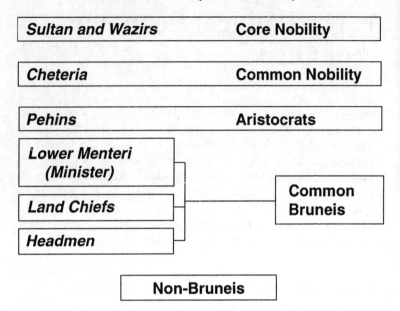

Figure 6.1   Social stratification in Brunei

followed through. The state-of-emergency legislation put into effect to deal with the crisis of 1962 remain in force. Criticism of the lack of apparent democracy is strongly countered by arguing that 'traditional' forms of representation within Malay culture are well-developed. Thus the *ketua kampong* (village head) and *penghulu mukim* (mukim, or district head) retain a degree of local power and, in theory, have access to the Sultan and government. Under revisions established in March 1992 the government has sought to establish a greater degree of accountability for these posts to try and ensure they represent local interests. A number of consultative councils for mukim and kampong leaders were also established as part of an elaborate plan to 'integrate government with leaders at the grass-roots … through which government decisions can be explained to the people and inputs received from the grass-roots leadership' (Mani, 1993, 99).

After independence, the 1959 Constitution remained in force and is the supreme law that provides the basic constitutional framework for the administration of the country. Some changes were made to acknowledge the new status of Brunei as a sovereign, independent country. A cabinet style of government was introduced, as noted in Chapter 2. The former offices of Chief Minister, State Secretary and State Financial Officer were abolished and replaced by new ministerial posts. Supreme executive authority is vested in the Sultan who is also Prime Minister, Minister of Defence and Supreme Commander of the Royal Brunei Armed Forces.

Cabinet has eleven members, each appointed by the Sultan. The Council of Ministers is presided over by the Sultan. The Religious Council advises the Sultan on matters relating to Islam; the Sultan is the Head of the Faith, which is the Shafeite sect. Religious freedom is enshrined in the Constitution; the recent emergence of more militant forms of Islam, together with more restrictive interpretations of the state religion have begun to test this constitutional freedom. Christian missionary activity, as well as prosyletising by more militant Islamic sects is discouraged. The Privy Council in Brunei advises the Sultan on constitutional matters. There is a Legislative Council but legislation is mainly enacted through Royal Proclamations. Traditionally, the tenets of English law were central to the legal system of Brunei. Stronger affinities to Islam has meant that there are moves to incorporate aspects of *Shariah* law into Brunei. In 1992, the system of seconding judges from Hong Kong to Brunei was abandoned. Historically the Sultan has always acted in consultation with his traditional advisers, principally the *wazirs*. These traditional advisers continue to play some part in government but no longer have a direct and clear involvement under the 1959 Constitution. The majority of them are members of the Privy Council and the Council of Succession. The Sultan also has a Special Adviser who is appointed as Minister of Home Affairs as well.

Such institutions, coupled with the local forms of representation highlighted earlier, reflect the strengthening of what have been termed traditional Malay forms of political representation. The need to reinforce traditional linkages between 'people' and 'government' have perhaps become more acute as economic modernisation and increased westernisation have taken effect in the state. Thus a range of often conflicting pressures — Islamic fundamentalism, western materialism, democratic reform, traditional notions of kingship — have underpinned recent political developments in Brunei. The conflicts and contradictions which have developed with the post-oil boom economic growth, has led to a heightened awareness of the interconnections between the economy

and polity of the state, and the role of development planning in helping
to achieve balanced, sustainable growth.

6.2   STATE IDEOLOGY

In both conceptual and administrative terms, discussions of development planning cannot be separated from the evolution of state ideology.
Given the absence of clear political accountability, the central role of the
Sultan, acting in Council, in ratifying decisions, and the complex networks linking the bureaucracy and the controlling interests in the state,
changing political ideologies have had important implications for the
role and character of development planning. One of the implicit functions of the development planning programme has been to help secure
the political functioning of the state. Thus, at one level, high spending
on social provision (free medical and educational provision; facilitating
attendance at the *haj*; public housing schemes) may be seen as essential
to securing a supportive populace. Similarly, diversification strategies
and employment-creating projects aim to reduce youth unemployment
and, hopefully mitigate the establishment of a non-work culture. Such
policies seek to secure both the political and economic future of the
state. Thus the objectives of development planning cannot be isolated
from the wider political ideologies pursued by the nation.

On independence, Brunei opted for a cabinet style of government;
ultimately, real executive power rests with the Sultan, who controls all
major decisions, and the Royal Family. The key positions (Prime Minister; Treasury; Foreign Affairs) in government are in the hands of the
Sultan and two of his brothers. The state is monarchical in style and
functions, with the ideology of the Malay Islamic Monarchy at its heart.
As Mulliner (1985, 215) has noted, 'despite the trappings of cabinet government, the predominance of the royal family in key posts demonstrates
the Sultan's committment to retaining a ruling rather than a figurehead
monarch which the Sultan likens to those of the Sultanate of Oman and
Saudi Arabia'. This structure has a number of consequences for the
development process. First, as was noted in Chapter 4 the distinction
between state finances and incomes, and royal finances and incomes, is
notoriously difficult to draw; royal assets and state assets remain inter-
twined. Investment incomes, in particular, are difficult to allocate into
one category or the other. Key institutions in Brunei — the Brunei

Investment Agency, the newly established Brunei Oil and Gas Authority, QAF Holdings or Primal Corporation are under close Royal control.

A second important consequence of the political system is that patron-client relations remain entrenched within the administrative system. Initiative and innovation is to a large extent stifled because of concerns that particular courses of action, particular decisions, might have adverse personal consequences. This is not to suggest that forms of corruption are widespread; there have been stringent efforts to ensure that corruption is minimal (the Anti-Corruption Bureau remains under the control of the Prime Ministers Office). Rather one can argue that the all-pervasive nature of a system of government based on royal prerogatives and patronage does not always facilitate open, objective and disinterested decision-making. Blunt's analysis (1988) of a particular educational institution in Brunei supports this view emphasising the latent conflicts between development 'demands' and the often rigid administrative structures. Brown (1984, 206) similarly has argued that 'the bureaucracies and the Councils are all linked in patron–client relationships with the ruler, so that no bureaucrat is really insulated from palace politics'.

The rapid economic growth experienced by the state since the first oil-price boom of 1973–4 has had important consequences for the ideological characteristics of the state. Economic growth has brought with it two contradictory trends: westernisation and Islamic fundamentalism. Increased personal and government incomes have facilitated much greater material prosperity; whilst income inequalities remain high, access to cars, air-conditioned houses, a lengthy education, consumer durables and international travel, are now commonplace, particularly amongst a growing middle class. Such materialism has however prompted fears that the 'westernisation' implied by development may undermine the Islamic traditions of the state and, by extension, the largely autocratic position enjoyed by the Sultan. At the same time, fundamentalist pressures from some Middle Eastern sources has become apparent. The fear that such fundamentalist pressures, articulated from more radical mosques, might undermine the position of the Sultan, has also been apparent. The banning in 1991 of the Islamic Jama'ah Al-Arquam movement, exemplifies such concerns.

At the same time, the state is profoundly Islamic in character; the banning of alcohol in 1990 and of pork production in 1992 suggest an increasing rigour in enforcing Islamic precepts. The Sultan, notes one observer (Anon, 1992, 128), 'finds legitimacy in religious charisma to which he responds — at least in the minds of believers — with acts of good faith, grand public works, and religious piety'. The visible performance of religious duties, attendance at the *Haj* and reinforcement of religious precepts through *titahs* typify such legitimising acts. In some respects, the ideology and visible symbolism of the state seems to reflect a balancing-act between 'western' and 'Islamic' pressures. Nowhere has this been more manifest than in the development of the state ideology of the Malay Muslim Monarchy which is likely to play an increasing role in the internal affairs and external positions — economic, political and social — of the country.

Whilst the nature and development of MIB have been fully described elsewhere (see, in particular, Braighlinn, 1992) some of the elements of the ideology are worth noting. MIB is based, first and foremost, on the centrality of history and tradition. Brunei, it is argued, has a long history as a sovereign state with one of the oldest royal families in the region. It is a Malay, Islamic state adopting Islam at an early stage, and committed, not to a multi-ethnic model of political and economic development as in the case of Malaysia, but rather to a uniquely Brunei Malay culture and polity. History, or to some observers, the invention of history, remains central to MIB. As Nicholl (1989) has noted, the full resources of the state History Centre have been devoted to elucidating the long traditions and glories of the royal line; such interpretations are, however, subject to some dispute.

Brunei, it is argued, has always been Malay, Islamic and monarchical in structure, and the role of MIB, first mooted in the late 1950s but flourishing from the late 1980s, is 'to theorise ideologically about today's political order (the Malay, Islamic monarchy) and then project this essence backwards in time' (Braighlinn, 1992, 29). Integral to this philosophy is the unquestioning position of the Sultan as ruler of the state, the centrality of Islam to the daily life of Brunei and an inherently cautious attitude to western ideas and values. MIB is seeking to establish a political and social philosophy which remains open to some aspects of the west (in this respect it is not fundamentalist in ethos) whilst continuing to be anchored to a Malay conception of monarch and people. One of the perhaps intended outcomes of MIB is that the absolute monarchy as an institution has become more pervasive than either Islam or malay culture.

The MIB philosophy is widely disseminated in Brunei. It thus forms an integral part of the education system, from primary through to university level. It is diffused widely through the press and state-controlled television. It is given visible substance in the elaborate court ceremonial surrounding events such as the Jubilee of the Sultan in late-1992. In his 1992 New Year message the Sultan underlined the importance of history and tradition: 'History has a role in resolving problems of the country. A race without its history is indigent. The celebration to be held this year is aimed to signify the importance of recording historical events for reference by future generations' (Mani, 1993, 95). Whilst ceremonial and protocol have always been integral to Malay culture, such events provide the opportunity to reinforce the central role of the monarchy.

In economic terms, MIB serves to reinforce a number of features of the distributive system. The linkage between state and royal finances is unproblematic, for the state is the family and the Sultan its father. Likewise the Sultan can be portrayed as the benevolent donor of funds: as Braighlinn (1992, 47) argues, 'economic development in itself is a tool of legitimation for the Sultan, and only by meeting current popular expectations can the Sultan justify his monopoly as "leader of development"'. MIB then, forms the ideological framework within which economic, social and development planning has emerged. Policies of diversification, of privatisation, of employment-creation can be seen both in terms of narrower economic objectives and the broader political economy of the state. Securing a stable economic base and sustainable development are essential if the political stability of the sultanate is to be assured. At present, MIB provides the ideological rationale for the current political structures of Brunei, and the critical context within which economic planning has developed. As one observer recently noted (Anon., 1992, 127–8), 'driven by conservatives in the ministries who are now riding high, the MIB ideology has, for all intents and purposes, become the touchstone for public policy as well as private demeanour in Brunei and has become the major test for loyalty'.

6.3 BRUNEI IN THE INTERNATIONAL ARENA

As a small state, Brunei's engagement in the international arena has been especially significant in increasing political legitimacy and international standing, and in creating a more secure and cooperative regional environment within which to function. Its international activities, undoubtedly bolstered by its wealth, have been focused in three areas:

bilateral ties, activity in the United Nations and the Commonwealth and, most importantly, membership of the Association of Southeast Asian Nations (ASEAN).

Brunei's bilateral ties have increased markedly over the last decade. Dominated by its strong links with Britain, in the immediate pre-independence period diplomatic functions were carried out through Brunei Government Agencies in London, Singapore and Kuala Lumpur. Those close diplomatic, educational and economic ties with the United Kingdom, Singapore and Malaysia remain. Strong links with Britain, in particular, still exist. The Sultan was Sandhurst-trained and remains Anglophile, despite the shifts in Bruneian political affinities with the development of MIB. Britain retains a form of military committment to Brunei through the Ghurka Batallion at Seria; the costs are, however, borne by the Sultan. British military personnel serve in an advisory capacity and Britain has access to jungle training facilities in the state. Large numbers of students continue to be sent to British colleges and universities for higher education.

Since independence, Brunei has established twenty permanent missions abroad with a further sixteen non-resident ambassadors accredited (Thambipillai, 1992, 284). Recent diplomatic ties with China and the Soviet Union reflect the process of detente in Southeast Asia as the Cambodian crisis has moved towards some sort of resolution. Some forty-three countries have diplomatic missions accredited to Brunei; eighteen of these have permanent missions in the capital. The annual opening of the United Nations Assembly in New York is traditionally used by Brunei to cement old ties and forge new ones, given that its resources for foreign relations work are finite. Brunei has not been averse to using its financial resources for international ends. The controversy surrounding a supposed gift to the Nicaraguan 'contras' in 1986 (Leake, 1990, 138–40), represents only the most-publicised case of using financial resources for international ends. The Sultan and state (whose funds are, in any case, imperfectly distinguished) have made gifts to the Palestinians, to Pakistan, to Muslim causes in Indonesia and Malaysia, and, most recently, to help the plight of Muslims in Bosnia.

Membership of international groups can provide major advantages for Brunei; as Thambipillai (1992, 282) has pointed out, 'group membership provides the support and confidence for participation in international diplomacy...the eight years of regional cooperation has contributed significantly to the strengthening of Brunei's role in its external affairs'. Brunei has been a powerful supporter of the British Commonwealth since becoming a full member on independence. Its closest regional neighbours and allies, Malaysia and Singapore are also active members, and the Commonwealth provides a range of technical and educational opportunities for Brunei as well as help in maintaining links with Australia, New Zealand, Canada and a range of Asian and African states. Brunei's financial contribution to the running of the Commonwealth is significant.

Brunei became a full member of the United Nations, the 159th, in September 1984. Through membership of the UN, Brunei seeks to reinforce the importance of collective security for small states such as itself. Similarly, given the finite resources available for diplomatic activity, the UN provides a convenient institutional focus through which diplomatic efforts can be efficiently channelled given the absence of a comprehensive diplomatic network. Finally Brunei is a full and active member of the forty-five member Organisation of Islamic Conference which reinforces solidarity with other Islamic states and provides Brunei with an input into international Islamic affairs.

6.4 BRUNEI AND ASEAN

Membership of ASEAN is perhaps the most important of these international linkages; it forms the cornerstone of its diplomatic activity. Brunei announced its intention of joining ASEAN in June 1981 and became a full member on 7 January 1984. Membership of ASEAN has provided Brunei with a number of advantages. Since the Emergency of 1962 and the period of 'konfrontasi' between Malaysia and Indonesia in the mid-1960s, the security of the country's borders has been a matter of concern. Relations with both Indonesia and Malaysia were rocky during the 1960s and 1970s because of concerns over Indonesian attitudes towards Brunei and the Federation of Malaysia, and because of tacit Malaysian support for some of the political activists of the 1962 rebellion. Membership of ASEAN has first and foremost greatly increased the territorial security of the state. It was Indonesia which provided the strongest support for Brunei's membership of ASEAN, a move which has helped to ease tensions over events in the mid-1960s and, perhaps more importantly, has allowed Brunei to redefine its relationship with Malaysia (Weatherbee, 1983, 730).

The relationship between Brunei and ASEAN has been a largely symbiotic one: 'it can retain a large measure of political security by becoming a member of ASEAN, without having to sacrifice its separate identity, share its oil revenues, or compromise its internal power structure' (Ranjit Singh, 1986, 171). For ASEAN Brunei's membership increases the prestige of the organisation and, perhaps more importantly, serves to defuse the potential for conflict over the territorial borders of the state. Potential conflict over such issues as the Limbang claim (Cleary and Shaw, 1992) or the Spratly Islands are much easier to resolve within the confines of ASEAN. Today ASEAN has become the cornerstone of Brunei's foreign policy. It is fully supportive of ASEAN policy towards the key issues in the region. Thus policy towards Cambodia has mirrored that of ASEAN and it has lent full support to the ZOPFAN concept (Zone of Peace, Freedom and Neutrality) for the Southeast Asian region. It has also supported the resolution of regional issues such as ownership of the Spratly Islands through the mediation of ASEAN rather than bilaterally. Other policy stands since independence — the withdrawal of Soviet troops from Afghanistan, the condemnation of apartheid in South Africa, support for the struggles of the Palestinian peoples — do not conflict with ASEAN membership.

In economic terms, membership of ASEAN has brought only minimal advantages to Brunei. Economic cooperation programmes in ASEAN have thus far made little progress. Given the overwhelmingly political objectives of ASEAN (Broinowski, 1990) it is perhaps not suprising that few direct and measurable economic benefits from membership are apparent. It is however likely that this position will change as the potential for an ASEAN Free Trade Area (AFTA) emerges. At a series of meetings in 1991 and 1992, member governments gave serious consideration to creating such a free trade area with agreement on establishing reductions on a range of traded products with a view to creating a free trade area over a 15-year time span (Imada and Naya, 1992). In 1990, about 28 per cent of Brunei's trade was with fellow ASEAN countries, a figure which was higher than any other ASEAN country. Admittedly, the bulk of that trade was in hydrocarbons and the AFTA provisions are unlikely to affect such products. However, given the focus on economic diversification in Brunei's economic strategy, the AFTA provisions may well have an effect (both positive and negative) on the success of that strategy.

The creation of ASEAN joint ventures and industrial complementarity projects has been perhaps the most visible form of cooperation. Brunei has benefited little from this; the pulp and paper project scheduled for the state has been abandoned. However Brunei remains committed to the concept of joint ventures within ASEAN. In 1991 it contributed $22 million to the ASEAN Corporation, set up to enhance cooperation between ASEAN states in the areas of agriculture, food and forestry.

Within ASEAN the ASEAN Council on Petroleum has established a mechanism for the sharing of crude oil between member states at times of crisis. Under a joint agreement, Malaysia, Indonesia and Brunei agreed to divert a proportion of their crude oil output to energy-deficient Thailand, Singapore and the Philippines whenever global oil shortages threaten regional supplies. The amount of crude supplied was determined by production capacity and the level of crude imports. Whilst the agreement has yet to be put into practice, 'the 1986...agreement is best recognised as a reaffirmation of the regional committment to use the regional framework to overcome immediate contingencies' (Rozali Mohamed Ali, 1987, 254).

In general Brunei's regional relationships have been greatly enhanced through membership of ASEAN. Relations with Malaysia have generally improved since the late 1970s. Historically, Brunei's refusal to join the Federation of Malaysia in 1963, and Malaysia's tacit support for the struggles of the Parti Rakyat Brunei in the 1962 rebellion created tensions in the relationship. The Limbang claim has also, on occasions, soured the relationships between the two states. However, with the approach of independence relations improved markedly with a series of visits between Brunei and Malaysia. By the early 1980s Malaysia was providing training and education facilities for Bruneian students and administrators and relations in the post-independence period have been good.

Brunei's relationship with Indonesia has similarly fluctuated. The Sukarno government gave support and refuge to the leaders of the 1962 Rebellion and it was not until the late-1970s, when Suharto declared his open support for Brunei's membership of ASEAN, that relationships improved. The Sultan paid an official visit to Indonesia in April 1981, and Indonesia has offered a range of training courses and facilities for Brunei military personnel. In 1987 the Sultan offered Indonesia a $100 million soft loan to finance a number of development schemes in the country. Economic and political linkages have greatly strengthened in recent years as ASEAN membership has blossomed.

The links between Singapore and Brunei have always been close and supportive, with both political and economic objectives. Both are small states, both have historically had concerns over territorial integrity, both share links with Britain. There are extensive trading links between the two states and much of the capital resources of Brunei are channelled through Singapore. The two currencies are interchangeable at parity. Brunei's financial resources are well complemented by Singapore's technical, commercial and investment acumen. Security links are also strong. Brunei military personnel receive training in Singapore whilst a Singapore Armed Forces infantry is stationed in the Temburong District for jungle training. Links with Thailand and the Philippines are generally weaker. Brunei imports large quantities of rice from the former as well as exporting increasing amounts of crude oil to that market. Both countries are very important sources of foreign labour.

Internationally, independence and membership of ASEAN has meant that Brunei plays a full role in international affairs consonant with its size and wealth. It is a full member of the United Nations and a full member of the Organisation of the Islamic Conference. Its nationals played a small role in peacekeeping operations in Cambodia in 1992 through membership of UNTAC. Both official and private donations to various causes (from the supposed donation to the Nicaraguan 'contras' in 1987 to donations to the Bosnian Muslims in 1992) are used to employ some of the wealth of the state for international, diplomatic ends.

6.5   TOWARDS A RENTIER STATE?

The excessive reliance of Brunei on one depletable revenue source has created particular developmental problems. These problems are similar to those of a number of other small, oil-producing states in the Middle East. In economic terms (reliance on non-renewable hydrocarbons; diversification strategies; high per capita GDP) Brunei is similar to Middle Eastern states such as Oman and Bahrain; similarities which also extend to size, to the central importance of Islam, and to avowedly 'traditional', monarchical systems of government. Many of these states have been characterised as 'rentier states'. These may be defined as countries that receive on a regular basis substantial amounts of external rent which are derived primarily from foreign sources (Beblawi and Giacomo, 1987).

In the case of Brunei, foreign investments constitute the lion's share of such rent, together with revenues accruing from hydrocarbon royalties and taxes. In the classic rentier state, the governments of these oil-exporting countries, together with the bulk of their citizens (as was noted in Chapter 3, direct employment in the oil-sector accounts for under 10 per cent of total state employment), often have little to do with the production processes of their major revenue-earners. The function of government is the sectoral allocation and social distribution of such revenues and rents. Saudi Arabia, notes Wilson (1979, 40), 'presents an almost perfect example of a rentier economy, a state with high consumption but little production, large incomes but no necessity to work for those earnings'.

These oil and rent revenues are essential to the social functioning of the rentier state. Not only do they permit the high earnings which can serve to ameliorate popular pressures for political reform, but they also enable government to embark on large public expenditure programmes which can be funded without direct taxation, and without creating major balance-of-payments problems. It is largely through the expenditure side that the economic control mechanisms of rentier societies function. A large percentage of GDP in such states depends on the consumption of depletable capital resources. High expenditure on the non-productive sector (e.g. defence expenditure on foreign equipment and technology; non-infrastructural public building projects; high social service expenditure) is a further characteristic (El Azhary, 1984, 12).

The emphasis given to longer-term development and economic planning in Brunei suggests that, rhetorically at least, the rentier-state option is not one that government seeks to follow (Gunn, 1993). In the preambles to the development plans, in government statements, and in the increasingly important *titahs* of the Sultan, the need for sustained and diversified development is stressed. There is, for example, real concern in government circles that the rentier-state option does not provide secure employment for a population which, though small, is growing rapidly. Youth unemployment is beginning to manifest itself in the Sultanate together with concerns that a non-work culture is developing. The political and social implications of rising unemployment are potentially serious. Pehin Rahman, appointed Minister of Industry and Primary

Resources in 1989, has explicitly articulated such concerns: 'We simply must diversify for otherwise the problems could be grave. We have got to create employment for the young — especially the new educated returning from abroad ... there are plenty of jobs around. But Bruneians are simply too choosy about what they'll do ... They prefer sitting at home, or just having a good badmington game. And, with our extended family system, they can afford to do it' (Weaver, 1991, 81–2). Such contradictions — wealth without development, income without the need for employment — are likely to lie at the heart of the development and diversification programmes upon which the future stability and security of the state will depend.

Conclusion

The major objective underlying this book, namely to link the evolution of the oil and gas industry in Brunei to the various ways in which development and diversification strategies have been pursued, has elicited a number of paradoxes. In particular, it has served to underline the disjuncture between economic growth and economic development. By the conventional standards of growth in gross domestic product, balance of payment figures or foreign reserves, Brunei has achieved impressive rates of economic growth, particularly since the first oil-price rises of 1973–4. But, as this book's examination of the development process in Brunei has shown, there remain major concerns about the lack of an effective and sustainable pattern of development in the state. Growth without development, wealth without employment might serve as a summary of those concerns. Some of the reasons — high public sector employment, the gaps in remuneration levels between private and public sectors, insufficient monitoring of development plans, and high levels of public spending — have been elucidated in this book.

The concern with development and employment issues is fundamental and far-reaching in both private and public discourse in the state. On what foundations is employment going to be based in the next twenty years? Given the finite nature of hydrocarbon resources, how is Brunei going to develop the strong, sustainable and diverse economy on which the future political stability of the state will depend? Where are the state revenues that are needed to maintain the high welfare provisions and consumption patterns that have characterised the last two decades going to come from? Given the high labour costs and infrastructural constraints that have operated in Brunei, much of the effort to develop and diversify has come through state planning. Whilst in recent years, the economic role of the state has perhaps begun to shift from that of providing employment opportunities, to facilitating their creation by other agencies and individuals, the central importance of state action remains axiomatic. If privatisation, diversification and Bruneianisation are the central motifs of government economic planning in the 1990s, the achievement of those aims continues to rest on the formulation of a range of development strategies. Such strategies, enshrined in the national development plans, have been the major focus of this book.

In reviewing the development and diversification programmes a number of problems make a clear judgement difficult. In particular, the problem of access to reliable, up-to-date data is a major problem inhibiting economic and social research. Undoubtedly the quality of information has greatly improved as better systems for monitoring the progress of development planning have been put in place. In addition there can be little doubt that the quality of planning personnel has also greatly improved over the last two decades. Such trends can only facilitate better planning and more coherent reviews and monitoring of particular planning programmes.

A preliminary assessment of the development programmes of the last two decades might well come up with somewhat mixed results. The impact of those programmes on employment has been limited. Most new employment in the state has been in the public sector where the majority of the working citizen population now work. The long-term sustainability of this large public sector depends on continued high revenues from the hydrocarbon sector which can hardly be guaranteed. Whilst Brunei does have reasonable reserves of oil and gas, the finite nature of those resources demonstrates, more clearly than anything else, the need for economic diversification. In addition, as Chapter 6 has emphasised, the political stability and security of the state also depends on successful diversification programmes if the problem of a 'non-work culture', alluded to by at least one senior minister, is to be averted.

Efforts at creating a viable agricultural sector to meet the growing demand for food (reflected in rising food imports) have not been a great success. In some sectors (poultry; egg production) there has been good progress; elsewhere, in rice or livestock production, for example, much needs to be done. In terms of employment-creation, it is unlikely that the current rate of progress in that sector will produce any dramatic results in the near future. A key problem, noted in Chapter 5, remains the gap between remuneration in the public and private sectors. This gap not only reduces the scope for shifting employment back into the agricultural sector, but also exercises real constraints on the expansion of private sector employment in manufacturing or services.

Developing a range of programmes to expand manufacturing and service employment has assumed an increasingly high priority in the last two development plans. Again, progress has been muted. Efforts to develop manufacturing have been thwarted by high labour costs: the traditional, small-scale workshop operation remains the archetypal form of factory employment in the state. Whilst that sector can remain productive, it is unlikely to be radically transformed to help secure future employment and growth. Preliminary results do at least suggest that some of the manufacturing developments, notably in the textile and food and beverage sector, are beginning to yield results. Service employment growth has been more impressive. The growth of retailing, banking and personal services has provided opportunities for job creation. Unfortunately, it has not always proved easy to attract Brunei citizens into a sector which tends to be less well paid than public service. In addition, it might be argued that the continued viability of that sector depends to an extent on the revenues generated by the hydrocarbon industry; the recycling of those revenues in the form of salary and welfare payments is the engine that has driven the expansion of employment in the tertiary sector.

Overall, then, as Chapters 4 and 5 have suggested, development planning and policies have had only limited success in achieving the aims of diversification, sustainable development and job creation. However, this somewhat negative conclusion needs to be qualified. It is clear that there have been major improvements in the elaboration, formulation and implementation of development and diversification strategies in Brunei. Economic planners now fully recognise the need to place diversification at the heart of development strategies; hydrocarbon revenues, it is now accepted, have to be used for development projects which will enhance the economic and employment prospects of a rapidly-growing population. The objectives and instruments of development planning have been greatly sharpened by the increasingly realistic reflections on the finite nature of the state's wealth. The dangers of Brunei becoming a state rich in income but poor in jobs and skills are increasingly stressed by planners and by the ruling elite alike. In addition, clear infrastructural improvements have been made in a number of areas ranging from education to telecommunications and public utilities.

If a first purpose of the book was to examine in detail the economy and planning infrastructure of Brunei, an ancillary aim was to seek to contextualise concepts of development and growth. In this respect, the present study will, it is hoped, have provided a wider frame of reference for an examination of state policy. As was noted in Chapter 4, the particular experience of Brunei can be seen as reflecting that of a number of other countries, especially in the Middle East. Issues such as the sustainability of oil revenues, their use for development and diversification purposes, the impacts of Dutch Disease phenomenon and the emergence of rentier states are far from unique to Brunei. Thus a range of wider development models and experiences can both reflect, and be reflected in, the experience of Brunei. Economic development, diversification policies and the organisation of the oil industry in Brunei have been shaped by a range of external influences and models. Indeed, for much of Brunei's contemporary history, it has been these external influences that have been paramount. The role of multi-national oil companies, the quasi-colonial links with Britain, the models and structures of development planning have all reflected, to a greater or lesser extent, outside influences.

It may well be in the shifting balance between external and indigenous influences on development issues that the wider interest of the Brunei case lies. As has been emphasised in Chapters 4 and 6, the emergence of the MIB philosophy can be read as an attempt to foster a more indigenous, Bruneian approach to questions of politics and economics. Whilst at the purely political level, it might be argued that MIB has served primarily as a tool for legitimation, its ramifications in the economic and social sphere are also significant. One of the underlying aspects of economic policy has been the tension between concepts of economic development which draw heavily from western conceptions of growth, equity and social justice, and aspects of the 'traditional' Brunei-Malay way of life where such concepts may be alien. Such tensions have been reflected in a number of ways: rising consumerism and the tenets of Islam, for example, or liberal, western educational traditions alongside Islamic religious schools, or an increasing involvement of women in the economy alongside the place of women in Islam.

It is such issues which provide the critical context within which the development programmes and experience of Brunei should be placed. Without that political, cultural and social context, it is largely impossible to understand the nature and dynamics of economic and social transformation in the state. Shorn of that context, any examination of development and diversification programmes in the state loses much of its meaning. It is in the interactions between the structures and evolution of the hydrocarbon economy, the objectives and mechanisms of development planning and the nature of the domestic and international political economy that the wider significance of the example of Brunei resides.

References

Ali, Sheikh, R. (1987) *Oil and Power: Political Dynamics in the Middle East,* London: Pinter.

Ameer Ali, A. (1992) 'Industrialization or Industries? The Vision and the Viability in Brunei Darussalam', *Universiti Brunei Darussalam Sumbangsih Sultan Hassanal Bolkiah Volume,* Universiti Brunei Darussalam, Brunei Darussalam.

Andaya, B. Watson and Andaya, Leonard (1982) *A History of Malaysia,* London: Macmillan.

Anderson, G. Bartlett, III, *et al.* (1972) *Pertamina: Indonesian National Oil,* Singapore: Amerasian Ltd.

Anon. (1992) 'Negara Brunei Darussalam in 1991: Relegitimizing Tradition', *Asian Survey,* XXXII, 2, pp. 126–30.

Anon. (1993) 'Brunei Darussalam in 1992: Monarchy, Islam and Oil', *Asian Survey,* XXXIII, 2, pp. 200–3.

Arief, Sritua (1982) *The Petroleum Industry and the Indonesian Economy: An Impact Study,* East Balmain, NSW: Rosecons.

Arief, Sritua (1986) *The Brunei Economy,* East Balmain, NSW: Rosecons.

ASEAN (1991) *Financial Systems of ASEAN member countries: the case of Brunei Darussalam,* Manila.

Asia Yearbook (1989, 1990, 1992) Hong Kong: Review Publishing Co. Ltd.

Attwood, James and Bray, Mark (1989) 'Wealthy but Small and Young: Brunei Darussalam and its Education', *Education Research and Perspectives,* 16, 2.

Azzam, H.T. (1988) *The Gulf Economies in Transition,* New York: St Martin's Press.

Banks, Ferdinand (1987) *The Political Economy of Natural Gas,* London: Croon Helm.

Beblawi, Hazem and Giacomo, Luciani (eds) (1987) *The Rentier State,* London: Croon Helm.

Bellwood, P. (1978) 'The Sultanate of Brunei', *Hemisphere,* 22, 11, pp. 18–23.

Bellwood, P. (1985) *Prehistory of the Indo-Malaysian Archipelago,* New South Wales: Academic Press.

Black, Ian (1983) *A Gambling Style of Government: The Establishment of Chartered Company Rule in Sabah, 1878–1915,* Kuala Lumpur: Oxford University Press.

Blunt, P. (1988) 'Cultural Consequences for Organization Change in a Southeast Asian State: Brunei', *Academy of Manpower Executive,* ii, 3, pp. 235–40.

Borneo Bulletin, Kuala Belait, various issues.

Braighlinn, G. (1992) *Ideological Innovation Under Monarchy: Aspects of Legitimation Activity in Contemporary Brunei,* Amsterdam: VU University Press.

Broinowski, Alison (ed.) (1990) *ASEAN into the 1990s,* Basingstoke: Macmillan.

Brown, D.E. (1970) *Brunei: The Structure and History of a Bornean Malay Sultanate,* Brunei: Brunei Museum Monograph.

Brown, D.E. (1984) 'Brunei on the Morrow of Independence' *Asian Survey,* XXIV, 2, pp. 201–208.

Brunei Darussalam Newsletter, Government of Brunei, various issues.

Brunei Shell (1985) *Annual Review*

Brunei Shell (1989) *Sixty Years On, 1929–89*

Bujang Bin Jumat (1989) Perindustrian di Negara Brunei Darussalam dan Kesannya terhadap Pekerjaan: Satu Kajian Kes di Muki Gadong. Unpublished Academic Exercise. Department of Geography. Universiti Brunei Darussalam.

Carlos, R. Clarita (1986) *Brunei In ASEAN: Problems and Prospects,* Paper presented at the 10th conference of the International Association of Historians of Asia (27–31 October 1986), Singapore.

Chi Seck Choo (1991) 'Industrialization in Brunei Darussalam: Problems and Prospects', in Voon Phin Keong *et al.* (eds), *The View From Within,* Kuala Lumpur: Malaysian Journal of Tropical Geography.

Chua Thia-Eng, Chou Loke Ming and Marie Sol M. Sadorra (1987) *The Coastal Environmental Profile of Brunei Darussalam: Resource Assessment and Management Issues,* Fisheries Department, Ministry of Development, Brunei Darussalam.

Cleary, Mark (1989) 'Some Themes in the Historical Geography of Coastal North-West Borneo', *Malaysian Journal of Tropical Geography,* 19, 7, pp. 7–14.

Cleary, Mark (1992a) 'Plantation Agriculture and the Development of Native Land Rights in British North Borneo c.1880–1930', *Geographical Journal,* vol. 158, 2, pp. 170–81.

Cleary, Mark (1992b) 'An Historical Geography of Brunei in the Early Residency Period, 1906–41' in *Universiti Brunei Darussalam Sumbangsih Sultan Hassanal Bolkiah Volume,* Universiti Brunei Darussalam: Brunei Darussalam, pp. 258–68.

Cleary, Mark (1994, forthcoming) 'Indigenous Trade and European Economic Intervention in North-West Borneo, c. 1860–1930', *Modern Asian Studies.*

Cleary, Mark and Eaton, Peter (1992) *Borneo: Change and Development,* Singapore: Oxford University Press.

Cleary, Mark and Kam Tin Seong (1992) 'The Changing Socio-Economic Structure of Kampong Ayer, Brunei Darussalam', *Malaysian Journal of Tropical Geography,* 22, 1, pp. 39–49.

Cleary, Mark and Shaw, Brian (1992) 'The Lost Province of Oil-Rich Brunei Darussalam', *Geography,* 1, pp. 178–81.

Cleary, Mark and Shuang Yann Wong (1993) 'Diversification Problems in a Rentier State: the case of Brunei', *Pacific Viewpoint,* 34, 1, pp. 69–76.

Colclough, Christopher (1985) 'Brunei: Development Problems of a Resource-Rich State', *Euro-Asia Business Review,* 4, pp. 29–32.

Cook, M. (ed.) (1970) *Studies in the Economic History of the Middle East,* London: Oxford University Press.

Corden, W.M. (1984) 'Booming Sector and Dutch Disease Economics: Survey and Consolidation', *Oxford Economic Papers,* 36, 3.

Corley, T.A.B. (1985) *A History of the Burmah Oil Company,* London: Heinemann.

Crisswell, C. (1972) 'Some Historical Aspects of Local and Sovereign Rights in Nineteenth-Century Brunei', *Journal of Oriental Studies,* 10, pp. 51–61.

Crystal, Jill (1990) Oil and Politics in the Gulf: Rulers and Merchants in Kuwait and Qatar, *Cambridge: Cambridge University Press.*

Cuddington, John (1989) 'Commodity Export Booms in Developing Countries', *World Bank Research Observer,* 4, 2, pp. 143–65.

Dassé, Martial (1991) 'Brunei: The Kuwait of South-East Asia', *Defense National,* 47, 135–49 (translated by Simon Francis).

Duraman Haji Ismail Bin Haji (1990) 'Income Distribution in Brunei Darussalam: A Macro Approach and Functional Expenditure Programmes', *Singapore Economic Review,* 35, 1, pp. 64–77.

Duke, John (ed.) (1975) *The Middle East: Oil, Politics and Development.* Washington: American Enterprise Institute for Public Policy.

Economic Development Board, Brunei Darussalam (1989) *Brunei Darussalam: Business in Perspective.*

Economic Development Board, Brunei Darussalam (1990) *Incentives for Investments in Brunei Darussalam.*

Economic Planning Unit (1974–90) *Brunei Darussalam Statistical Yearbook,* Ministry of Finance, Brunei Darussalam.

Economic Planning Unit (1977) *Third National Development Plan, 1975–9.* Star Trading and Printing.

Economic Planning Unit (1980) *The Fourth National Development Plan, 1980–4,* Brunei Darussalam: State Secretariat.

Economic Planning Unit (1985) *The Fifth National Development Plan, 1986–90,* Brunei Darussalam: Ministry of Finance.

Economic Planning Unit (1993) *The Sixth National Development Plan, 1991–5,* Brunei Darussalam: Ministry of Finance.

Economist Intelligence Unit *Economist Country Survey: Malaysia and Brunei,* Quarterly Reports, London: The Economist.

El Azhary, M.S. (1984) (ed.) *The Impact of Oil Revenues on Arab Gulf Development,* London: Croom Helm.

Energy Information Administration (1984) *The Petroleum Resources of Indonesia, Malaysia, Brunei and Thailand,* Washington, D.C.: US Department of Energy.

Farid, A.M. (1981) *Oil and Security in the Arabian Gulf,* London: Croom Helm.

Fisher, W.B. (1978) *The Middle East,* London: Methuen.

Francis, Simon (1993) *Pictures of the Palace: Travellers' Accounts of the Brunei of Sultan Abdul Momin and Sultan Hassan Between 1881 and 1906,* Hull: University of Hull Centre for South-East Asian Studies, Occasional Paper 23.

Franz, Johannes C. (1980) *The Sultanate of Brunei: Oil Wealth and Problems of Development,* Nuernberg: Wirtschafts und Sozialgeographisches Institut der Friederich-Alexander-Universitaet (translated by M.Schmitz and A.Sharp).

Fulton, S.J. (1984) 'Brunei: Past and Present', *Asian Affairs,* 15 (1). pp. 5–14.

Gelb, A., *et al.* (1988) *Oil Windfalls: Blessing or Curse?* New York: Oxford University Press.

Gerretson, F.C. (1958) *History of the Royal Dutch,* Leiden: Brill E.J.

Giacomo, Luciani (1984) *The Oil Companies and the Arab World,* London: Croom Helm.

Gill, Ian (1980) 'Shell loses its Brunei Monopoly', *Insight,* October, pp. 45–50.

Goh Kim Chuan (1992) 'Environmental Management', *Singapore Journal of Tropical Geography,* 13, 1, pp. 14–24.

Gunn, Geoffrey (1993) 'Rentier Capitalism in Negara Brunei Darussalam', in R. Robinson, K. Hewison, G. Rodan (eds), *Southeast Asia in the 1990s — Authoritarianism, Democracy and Capitalism,* Sydney: Allen and Unwin.

Hamzah, B.A. (1980) *Oil and Economic Development Issues in Brunei,* Singapore: Institute of Southeast Asian Studies, Research Notes and Discussion Paper 14.

Hamzah, B.A. (1992) *The Oil Sultanate: Political History of Oil in Brunei Darussalam,* Seremban: Mawaddah Enterprise Sdn. Bhd.

Hardstone, Peter (1978) 'Protected State or New Nation? Brunei: A Case Study in Political Geography', *Tijdschrift voor Econ. en Soc. Geografie,* 69, 3, pp. 165–71.

Harper, G. (1975) *The Discovery and Development of the Seria Oilfield,* Brunei: Brunei Museum Monograph.

Harrisson, T. (1970) *The Malays of South West Sarawak before Malaysia,* London: Macmillan.

Hon Kong Tse and Nicholas Fernandes (1991) 'Oil and Economic Development in the Sultanate of Brunei' In Sadri Sorab (ed.), *Oil and Economic Development,* Kuala Lumpur: Forum.

Horton, A.V.M. (1984) *The British Residency in Brunei, 1906–59,* Hull: University of Hull Centre for Southeast Asian Studies, Occasional Paper 6.

Horton, A.V.M. (1985) 'The Development of Brunei during the British Residential Era, 1906–1959', PhD Thesis, University of Hull.

Horton, A.V.M. (1987) 'The Disturbances in the Tutong and Belait Districts of Brunei, 1899–1901', *Journal of Southeast Asian Studies,* 18, 1, pp. 93–107.

Horton, A.V.M. (1988) 'Brunei, 75 Years Ago', *Sarawak Gazette,* CXV, pp. 14–20.

Horton, A.V.M. (1990) 'Brunei, 50 Years Ago', *Sarawak Gazette,* CXVII, pp. 15–23.

Hussainmiya, Haji B.A. (1992) 'Some Aspects of Social and Political Development in Brunei Darussalam, 1950–1959: the role of Al-Marhum Sultan Haji Omar Ali Saifuddien III', in *Universiti Brunei Darussalam Sumbangsih Sultan Hassanal Bolkiah Volume,* Universiti Brunei Darussalam: Brunei Darussalam pp. 164–82.

Huszar Brammah and Associates (1986) *Brunei Darussalam Master Plan.*

Huxley, Tim (1987) 'Brunei: Defending a Mini State' In Chin Kin Wah (ed.) *Defence Spending in Southeast Asia,* Singapore: Institute of Southeast Asian Studies.

Imada, Pearl and Naya, Seiji (eds) (1992) *AFTA: The Way Ahead,* Singapore: Institute of Southeast Asian Studies, ASEAN Economic Research Unit.

Jones, Geoffrey (1981) *The State and the Emergence of the British Oil Industry,* London: Macmillan.

Jones, Peter Ellis (1988) *Oil: A Practical Guide to the Economics of World Petroleum,* Cambridge: Woodhead Faulkner.

Jones, L.W. (1966) *The Population of Borneo: A Study of the Peoples of Sarawak, Sabah and Brunei,* London: Athlone Press.

Kelly. J.B. (1980) *Arabia, the Gulf and the West,* New York: Basic Books.

Kershaw Roger (1984) 'Illuminating The Path to Independence: Political Themes in Pelita Brunei in 1983', *Southeast Asian Affairs 1984,* Singapore: Institute of Southeast Asian Studies.

Khoo Soo Hock *et al.* (1976) *Brunei In Transition: Aspects of Its Human Geography in the Sixties,* Department of Geography Occasional Paper No. 2. Kuala Lumpur.

King, Terry (ed.) (1992) *The Best of Borneo Travel,* Singapore: Oxford University Press.

Leake, David (1990) *Brunei: The Modern Southeast-Asian Islamic Sultanate.* Kuala Lumpur: Forum.

Liesl, Graz (1990), *The Turbulent Gulf,* London: Tauris.

Lim, David (1990) 'Economic Adjustments under Conditions of Abundance: Implications for Malaysia and Sabah', *Borneo Review,* 1, 1, pp. 149–59.

Lindblad, J.Th. (1988) *Between Dayak and Dutch: The Economic History of Southeast Kalimantan. 1880–1942,* Dordrecht: Foris Publications.

Longhurst, H.C. (1956) *The Borneo Story: The History of the First One Hundred Years of Trading in the Far East,* London: Newman Neame Ltd.

Longhurst, H.C. (1959) *Adventure in Oil. The Story of British Petroleum.* London: Sidgwick and Jackson.

Looney, Robert E. (1991) 'Diversification in a Small Oil Exporting Economy: The Impact of the Dutch Disease on Kuwait's Industrialization', *Resources Policy,* March, 31–41.

Mahdavy, H. (1970) 'The Pattern and Problems of Economic Development in rentier States: The Case of Iran' in M Cook (ed) *Studies in the Economic History of the Middle East,* London: Oxford University Press.

Mani, A. (1993) 'Negara Brunei Darussalam in 1992: Celebrating the Silver Jubilee', *Southeast Asian Affairs 1993,* Singapore: Institute of Southeast Asian Studies, pp. 95–112.

Mansfield, Peter (ed.) (1980) *The Middle East: A Political and Economic Survey,* New York: Oxford University Press.

McArthur, Malcolm (1987) *Report on Brunei in 1904.* Athens, Ohio: Monographs in International Studies: SEA Series, 74.

Menon, K.U. (1987) 'Brunei Darussalam In 1986: In Search of the Political Kingdom', *Southeast Asian Affairs 1988,* Singapore: Institute of Southeast Asian Studies, pp. 85–101.

Menon, K.U. (1989) 'Brunei Darussalam in 1988: Ageing in the Wood', *Asian Survey* XXIX. 2, pp. 140–4.

Ministry of Development (1986) Negara Brunei Darussalam Master Plan, Background Paper, Manpower, unpublished report.

Ministry of Development (1986) Negara Brunei Darussalam Master Plan, Background Paper, Crop Production, unpublished report.

Moehammad Nazir (1990) 'Income Distribution in Brunei Darussalam:The Case of Kampong Ayer', *Singapore Economic Review,* 35, 2.

Moehammad Nazir (1992) 'Pelaburan di Negara Brunei Darussalam: Arah Aliran 1975–1985 Dan Pencepat Pelaburan' In *Universiti Brunei Darussalam Sumbangsih Sultan Hassanal Bolkiah Volume,* Universiti Brunei Darussalam: Brunei Darussalam pp. 206-16.

Morrisson, H. (1951) 'Brunei and the Seria Oilfields', *New Commonwealth,* April, pp. 498–501.

Mulliner, K. (1985) 'Brunei in 1984: Business as Usual After the Gala', *Asian Survey,* XXV, 2, pp. 214–219.

Neary, J. Peter and Van Wijnbergen, Sweder (1986) *Natural Resources and the Macroeconomy,* Cambridge, Mass: MIT Press.

Neville, Warwick (1985) 'Economy and Employment in Brunei', *Geographical Review,* 75, 4, pp. 451–61.

Neville, Warwick (1990) 'The Population Composition of Brunei', *Singapore Journal of Tropical Geography,* 11, 1, pp. 27–42.

Nicholas, David (1981) *The Middle East: Its Oil, Economies and Investment Policies,* London: Mansell.

Nicholl, Robert (ed.) (1975) *European Sources for the History of the Sultanate of Brunei in the Sixteenth Century,* Brunei Darussalam: Brunei Museum.

Nicholl, Robert (1989) 'Some Problems of Brunei Chronology', *Journal of Southeast Asian Studies,* XX, 2, pp. 175–95.

Niew Shong Tong (1989) *Demographic Trends in Negara Brunei Darussalam,* Universiti Brunei Darussalam, Brunei Darussalam.

Nugent, Jeffrey and Thomas, Theodore (eds) (1985) *Bahrain and the Gulf: Past Perspectives and Alternative Futures,* London: Croon Helm.

Odell, Peter (1975) *Oil and World Power,* Harmondsworth: Penguin

Ong Teck Mong, Timothy (1983) 'Modern Brunei: Some Important Issues', *Southeast Asian Affairs,* Singapore: Institute of Southeast Asian Affairs.

Ooi Jin Bee (1982) *The Petroleum Resources of Indonesia,* Kuala Lumpur: Oxford University Press.

Osama, Abdul Rahman (1987) *The Dilemma of Development in the Arabian Peninsula,* London: Croon Helm.

Peterson, J.E. (1983) *The Politics of Middle Eastern Oil,* Washington: Middle East Institute.

Pelita Brunei, Government of Brunei, various issues.

Quazi Abdul Halim (1992) 'Geological Resources', Singapore Journal of Tropical Geography, 13, 1, pp. 38–51.

Ranjit, Singh (1984) *Brunei 1839–1983: The Problems of Political Survival,* Singapore: Oxford University Press.

Ranjit, Singh (1986) 'Brunei in 1985: Domestic Factors, Political and Economic Externalities', *Asian Survey,* XXVI, 2, pp. 168–73.

Rolt, S.C. and Talib, H. (1986) 'Brunei', in *Income Taxation in ASEAN*. Singapore: Asian/Pacific Tax and Investment Centre.

Rozali, Moh. Ali (1987) 'Enhancing ASEAN economic cooperation in energy', in Noordin Sopiee *et al.* (ed.), *ASEAN at the Crossroads*, Kuala Lumpur: ISIS. pp. 251–261.

Sampson, Anthony (1975) *The Seven Sisters*, New York: Viking Press.

Selvanathan Subramaniam (1992) 'Fishery Resources', *Singapore Journal of Tropical Geography*, 13, 1, pp. 52–62.

Shankar, Sharma (1989) *The Role of the Petroleum Industry in Singapore's economy*, Singapore: Institute of Southeast Asian Studies.

Shankar, Sharma. (1991) *Energy Markets and Policies in ASEAN*, Singapore: Institute of Southeast Asian Studies.

Shankar, Sharma and Tan, Joseph (eds) (1991) *Global Oil Trends: The Asia-Pacific in the 1990s*, Singapore: Institute of Southeast Asian Studies.

Sheikh, R.A. (1987) *Oil and Power: Political Dynamics in the Middle East*, London: Pinter.

Siddayao Corazon Morales (1980a) *The Offshore Petroleum Resources of Southeast Asia*, Kuala Lumpur: Oxford University Press.

Siddayao Corazon Morales (1980b) *The Supply of Petroleum Reserves in Southeast Asia*, Kuala Lumpur: Oxford University Press.

Siddique, Sharon (1986) 'Brunei Darussalam in 1985: A Year of Nation-Building' in *Southeast Asian Affairs 1986*, Singapore: Institute of Southeast Asian Studies.

Siddique, Sharon (1992) 'Brunei Darussalam: The Non-Secular Nation', in *Southeast Asian Affairs 1992*, Singapore: Institute of Southeast Asian Studies.

Sinclair, Stewart (1984) *The World Petroleum Industry: The Market for Petroleum and Petroleum Products in the 1980s*, New York: Facts on File Publications.

Sorab Sadri (ed) (1991) *Oil and Economic Development*, Kuala Lumpur: Forum.

State of Brunei (1953) *Five Year Development Plan (1954–1958), Summary of Proposals*.

State of Brunei (1962) *Second National Five Year Development Plan (1962–6)*.

State of Brunei *Brunei Annual Reports* (various years, 1908–1990), Brunei: Government Printer.

State of Brunei Report on the Census of Population 1971.

State of Brunei Report on the Census of Population 1981.

Tarling, N. (1966) *South East Asia: Past and Present*, Melbourne: Cheshire.

Tarling, N. (1993) *The Fall of Imperial Britain in South-East Asia*, Singapore: Oxford University Press.

Tate, D.J.M. (1971) The Making of Modern South-East Asia, Vol. 1. Kuala Lumpur: Oxford University Press.

Todaro, Michael P. (1989) *Development Planning: Models and Methods*, New York: Oxford University Press.

Thambipillai, Pushpa (1982) 'Brunei in ASEAN', in *Southeast Asian Affairs,*1982, Singapore: Institute of Southeast Asian Studies.

150   *References*

Thambipillai, Pushpa (1990) *Foreign Workers and Development in ASEAN: The Brunei Context,* Universiti Brunei Darussalam: Department of Public Policy and Administration Working Paper.

Thambipillai, Pushpa (1992) 'Diplomacy and the Small State: Brunei Darussalam and the International System', *Sumbangsih UBD: Esei-Esei Mengenai Negara Brunei Darussalam,* pp. 276–290.

Stevens, Christopher (1982) *Nigeria, Economic Prospects to 1985: After the Oil Glut,* London: Economist Intelligence Unit.

Turnbull, C. Mary (1981) *A Short History of Malaysia, Singapore and Brunei,* Singapore: Graham Brash.

Valencia, Mark J. (1985) *Southeast Asian Seas: Oil under Troubled Waters: Hydrocarbon Potential, Jurisdictional Issues and International Relations,* Singapore: Oxford University Press.

Venn, Fiona (1986) *Oil and Diplomacy in the Twentieth Century,* Basingstoke: Macmillan.

Wade, G.P. (1986) 'Po-Luo and Borneo: A re-examination', *Brunei Museum Journal,* 6, 2, pp. 13–35.

Warren, J.F. (1981) *The Sulu Zone,* 1768–1898, Singapore: Singapore University Press.

Waterson, Albert (1972) *Development Planning: Lessons of Experience,* Baltimore: Johns Hopkins University Press.

Weaver, Mary-Ann (1991) 'Our Far-Flung Correspondents: In the Sultan's Palace', *The New Yorker,* 7/10/91.

Weatherbee, Donald E. (1983) 'Brunei: The ASEAN Connection', Asian Survey, XXIII, 6, pp. 723–735.

Wilford, G.E. (1961) The Geology and Mineral Resources of Brunei and Adjacent Parts of Sarawak with Descriptions of Seria and Miri Oilfields, State of Brunei.

Wijeweera, Bernard (1992) 'Administrative Development in Brunei Darussalam, 1950–90: A Survey in Historical Perspective' in *Universiti Brunei Darussalam Sumbangsih Sultan Hassanal Bolkiah Volume,* Universiti Brunei Darussalam, Brunei Darussalam, pp. 183–95.

Wilson, Rodney (1979) *The Economies of the Middle East,* London: Macmillan.

Wimalatissa, W.A. (1992) 'Enterpreneurial Characteristics and Business Performance of Small Business Owners and Managers: A Case Study of Beribi Industrial Complex, Gadong', in *Universiti Brunei Darussalam Sumbangsih Sultan Hassanal Bolkiah Volume,* Universiti Brunei Darussalam, Brunei Darussalam, pp. 217–36.

Wong, Shuang Yann (1993) *The Forgotten Sector in an Oil-Rich Economy: Agriculture in Brunei Darussalam,* V.R.F.Series No.210, Tokyo: Institute of Developing Economies.

Yergin Daniel (1991) *The Prize: the Epic Quest for Oil, Money and Power,* New York: Simon and Schuster.

Zainal Kling (1990) 'The Changing International Image of Brunei', in *Southeast Asian Affairs 1990,* Singapore: Institute of Southeast Asian Studies, Singapore, pp. 89–100.

Index